Robin Williams

HAND MADE

DESIGN WORKSHOP
CREATE HANDMADE ELEMENTS FOR DIGITAL DESIGN

Carmen Sheldon & Robin Williams

Robin Williams
Handmade Design Workshop: Create Handmade Elements for Digital Design
Carmen Sheldon and Robin Williams
Copyright ©2010 Carmen Sheldon and Robin Williams

Peachpit Press
1249 Eighth Street
Berkeley, CA 94710
510.524.2178 voice
510.524.2221 fax

Find us on the web at www.peachpit.com
To report errors, please send a note to errata@peachpit.com
Peachpit Press is a division of Pearson Education

Editors: Robin Williams and Nikki McDonald
Proofreader: Barbara Riley and Nikki McDonald
Photographers: Greg Sheldon and John Tollett
Cover design: John Tollett
Interior design and production: Robin Williams
Compositor: Robin Williams
Indexer: Robin Williams

ISBN 13: 978-0-321-64715-3
ISBN 10: 0-321-64715-7
10 9 8 7 6 5 4 3 2 1
Printed and bound in the United States of America

*scratchboard illustration
and wine label,
by Kim Rossiter Bernardi*

To Greg. Thank you, my love.

To my parents, Donal and LaVerne Richert
who showed me the world. I will miss you.
~Carmen

To Carmen Sheldon, Barbara McNally, Kathy Thornton—
I miss teaching with you at the JC!
~Robin

Contents

Introduction, *from Robin* 7

Why this book? *from Carmen* 8

Materials   11

1   Surfaces on which to Create 12

2   Stuff to Put on your Surfaces 16

3   Transfer an Image to a Surface 20

4   Heat, Cut, Score, Perforate 22

5   Adhesives—Glue it Down 26

Texture your Surface   31

6   Crackle the Surface 34

7   Texturize with Modeling Paste 38

8   Create a Patina 42

9   Peel the Paint 46

10 Rub and Rag the Paint 50

11 Stamp Textures with Alcohol Inks 56

12 Texturize with Absorbent Ground
     and Washi Paper. 60

13 Make Textures with Monoprints 66

14 Make Textures with Bubbles. 70

     Combine Techniques!. 72

Paint Textures   73

15 Salt the Paint 76

16 Blow the Paint 78

17 Spray the Paint 80

18 Pour the Paint 82

Carmen used a watercolor salt texture to simulate birds flying across the sky in this piece for her parents' presentation.

19   Scratch the Paint 86

20   Sponge the Paint 90

21   Splatter the Paint 94

22   Paint with Resist 98

23   Stamp-Resist into the Paint 102

24   Bleach the Paint 106

25   Tape and Paint 110

26   Plastic Wrap and Paint 112

27   Paper Towels and Paint 114

     Combine Techniques! 116

Paper & Metal Projects 117

28   Marble the Paper 120

29   Collage with Paper 124

30   Collage with Metal 134

31   Make your own Paper 140

32   Cast Paper 3D Images 150

33   Blind-Emboss the Paper 156

34   Gold-Stamp the Paper 160

35   Metal-Leaf an Image 162

36   Emboss with Powders 164

     Combine Techniques! 168

Illustrative Techniques 169

37   Scratch into Scratchboard 172

38   Illustrate with Found-Object Art 178

39   Illustrate with Clay 186

40   Illustrate with Collage 196

41   How to Draw if you can't Draw 198

Printing & Transfers 205

42   Roller Printing 208

43   Stamp Printing 210

44   Printmaking 214

     With Rubber Carving Blocks 216

     With Linoleum Blocks 220

     With Wood Blocks 222

     With Found Objects 224

45   Transfer Images 226

     Transfer to Polymer Backing 227

     Transfer Directly to Substrate 228

     Transfer with Lazertran 230

     Transfer with Packing Tape 231

Appendix: Resources 232

*Robin illustrated this wedding invitation
for typographers with mosaics.*

Thank you!

Carmen, thank you for allowing me into this book! I am honored that you choose to include it in the Design Workshop series. I must say, after having written and designed more than sixty books, I've never had so much fun or felt so satisfied and happy while working on any book. It was pure delight! *Thank you!*

And thanks to my Sweet Heart, John Tollett, for patiently shooting and Photoshopping hundreds of photos out of the kindness of your Big Beautiful Heart, and for making examples when Carmen and I were totally frazzled. What would I do without you?

And Nikki McDonald (editor), Barbara Riley (proofer), and David Van Ness (pre-press)—thanks for your stupendous work! *~Robin*

There are many people who encouraged me to realize my goal to write a book. My dear friend, Robin Williams, who writes huge tomes about computers for Peachpit Press, has always tried to get me to write books. But I felt I had nothing to add to the plethora of volumes on creating good-looking graphics.

However, I could never find a book that covered all the techniques I teach my students that don't involve digital applications—now there was a niche I could fill. Along came a chance for sabbatical and all of a sudden I was granted that precious commodity—time. I took advantage of the afternoons after my Spanish lessons in South America to type away on my laptop. There was something familiar and comforting in writing about my favorite art supplies and techniques in the middle of foreign cities.

My long-suffering husband, Greg, dutifully studied his Spanish lessons while I typed on. I could tell that he wished I was a little more excited about my Spanish verb conjugations than texture techniques using modeling paste, but he always made sure I had time to complete another chapter. Greg even agreed to the arduous task of photographing all my step-by step demos. I owe him tons for his patience, encouragement, and hard work.

When I finally was close to finishing my draft, I showed it to Robin and suggested tentatively that it might be a great addition to her Design Workshop series. She enthusiastically agreed. Robin and her talented sweetheart, John, helped me through the unfamiliar territory of publishing, helped package all my pieces into a stunning book, added additional information and beautiful design examples. I couldn't have done it without them. Thanks, you two. I love you to pieces.

I have to acknowledge my wonderful graphic design teacher, Max Hein. He inspired me greatly. And I learned so much from him.

Of course, my students are the real inspiration for this book. I wanted to put the information together in a way that they could refer to as they work on their projects. They have encouraged me, taught me new techniques, and even contributed to my book. Teaching an enthusiastic class is a wonderful experience.

I also want to acknowledge my manicurist, Susan Doan. As an artist, my hands and nails usually look rather abysmal. Susan helped me look more presentable for all those photographs. Thanks, my dear.

And thank you, Peachpit, for taking a chance on a book that steps outside of technology a tad. You have been so supportive, Nikki, and I appreciate all the behind-the-scenes efforts of David and Barbara as well.

~Carmen

Introduction *from Robin*

Carmen and I have known each other for more than thirty years. We've gone through school, small businesses, marriages, births, deaths, divorces, new partners, foreign countries, and teenagers together.

You'd think we're probably somewhat alike, but we're as different as can be, and I think you'll notice that in this book. For one thing, Carmen is a skilled illustrator and watercolorist; I'm terrified of paint brushes unless it's to paint the side of a house. So where Carmen gives you an elegant, controlled, lovely example, I often provide the sloppy, fast, scared-of-paintbrush version. Thus you can choose from both worlds and mix them up together to create your own scared, sloppy, elegant, lovely work.

But then, maybe you've already been dabbling in the handmade arts? Me too. Just before Carmen approached me with her book, I realized that I had begun working handmade techniques into many of my own projects, most specifically my *Shakespeare Papers,* small 20-page booklets that

I publish every two months, each one designed completely differently (TheShakespearePapers.com). For instance, I used my mosaic skills for illustrations, studied bookbinding to create my own miniature books, and resolved to learn the art of wood engraving. Then I discovered it wasn't just me—that throughout the design world there is a hankering to get away from the computer and use our hands again.

Carmen has been way ahead of this trend—for years she has taught a class for her digital design students in which they never touch a computer. By the end of the class, students discover they are better *digital* designers once they expand their treasury of creative tools to include those that have nothing to do with a computer at all, such as making paper, splattering paint, and modeling clay. This book is a result of her class.

Thus this is Carmen's book—I just helped. It's her voice you hear

throughout the pages; whenever I pipe up or wherever it might be unclear who's speaking, I've put one of our initials so you know which one of us is talking.

Carmen and I may be very different, but we both believe that it's time to expand your possibilities as a digital designer and learn new ways to create work that's uniquely yours. This means put down your mouse, grab a brush, and play a little dirty!

Why this book?

Why write a book like this in the digital age? After all, there are numerous web sites with textures, photos, illustrations, and fonts to be had for free or a pittance. Why would any designer want to make a textured background herself and ruin a perfectly good manicure? Isn't it true that to be a good designer in this slick, tidy age we need only a Visa card, some great links, and a mastery of Photoshop?

No. Trust me, I adore my Mac to the point of obsession. But as a designer and instructor, I do lament the sameness of so much of the design that appears when we're not willing to shut off our precious machines, push back our ergonomic chairs, pull out some of our dusty art supplies, and make something original that has our bit of humanity stamped in its bones.

I am not advocating that our digital tools be tossed and we go back to the days of rubber cement and rubylith. What I encourage is for a designer to work with some physical materials, digitize that piece, flesh it out with sensitive, effective typography, and create something truly unique.

So many of the trends and popular techniques we all use today had a genesis in handmade craftsmanship, and now we turn backflips trying to recreate those looks and effects with our software. Today's designer needs to look up and see the world in all its gorgeous shabbiness as inspiration to create visual graphics that communicate to a vast and diverse audience. Keeping one's nose within twelve inches of a computer screen only ensures a sameness in design that lacks any human connection or modern relevance.

No site on the web inspires me like a visit to a modern art show at SF MOMA. No amount of Internet research provides the impact of a boat ride between the towering skyscrapers of Chicago. Not even the design annuals have the tactile feel of a piece of kente cloth from Ghana. All of these experiences provide material for your work. They give you ideas that are different and original. If you make an effort to be creative, curious, and a pack rat of visual stuff, when the time comes to pull out all the creative stops, you will be a virtual cauldron bubbling over with ideas and concepts.

During my sabbatical in South America, I had the pleasure of visiting the home of the Chilean poet laureate, Pablo Neruda, in Isla Negra. I'm always fascinated with how creative people live. I'm curious how they mix everyday living with their passion. Neruda's home made a big impression on me. I felt a kindred spirit in the way he surrounded himself with the oddest things that then became inspiration for his poetry. He collected everything— old glass foot holders for pianos, worn-out ceramic bed warmers, figure heads from old ships, bugs, shells. He termed himself a "cosista" (a word he invented) rather than a collector because he felt a collector collects one thing and is always looking for the best of that item, while the cosista collects anything and everything that fascinates, whether or not it is valuable or in pristine condition.

I found a soulmate in Neruda. I collect stuff. Not to the extent Neruda did, but I do collect stuff. A few art papers here and there, ephemera I pick up in the oddest places, some textiles, folk art.

But mostly I collect ideas that I keep in my vast collection of journals—sketches of anything that interests me, little graphics I glue in, inspiring quotes, techniques from contemporary fine art that I then want to use for graphic design.

With this book, I hope to inspire you to become a cosista of ideas. I want to inspire you to look at your big, wide world, try it all, and become a true original.

Art like Life is a messy, sloppy, gooey infusion of enthusiasm & creativity.

Fred B. Mullett

PART 1

Materials

Materials are an essential part of the equation when it comes to creating handmade elements. My own experience with the success or failure of a particular technique has often hinged on the materials I chose. I hated scratchboard until I found Esdee Scraper Board from England; watercolor painting was almost a chore until I discovered 300 lb. Arches cold press paper; tracing on paper was frustrating until I used 90 lb. Vidalon from Canson. In some aspects of my career I can easily use just about anything at hand to get the job done (including a PC), but in some areas I am a complete elitist and only the best will do.

Find a few favorite products to always keep on hand—if you like your materials, you will be more likely to use them.

1 Surfaces on which to Create

In this chapter

- Bond paper
- Tracing paper
- Layout and visualizing paper
- Printing paper
- Art paper
- Watercolor paper
- Canvas
- Bristol board
- Masonite
- Clayboard
- Plexiglass
- Chipboard

One of the reasons I became a print designer is my fascination with and absolute love of papers and other surfaces. I love their smell, their feel, and their visual appeal. I collect papers wherever I go and keep them in large drawers in my studio. I use my collection for collages, backgrounds, inspiration, mockups, and more. Often a project will start with just a sheet of amazing paper.

However, choosing the wrong paper or surface for a project can cause great frustration. It's important to experiment, ask questions, learn about the qualities of the material you plan to use.

I have worked with numerous types of surfaces and papers and, of course, have developed some pretty specific preferences. I encourage you to become a student of papers and surfaces. Experiment with your finds. Be on the lookout for new products. Ask lots of questions. And organize your collection in a manner that protects your investment and keeps these items within easy reach.

Terms

Substrate refers to whatever you're putting your art onto. Your substrate might be paper, masonite, acetate, cardboard, tile, a wall, a t-shirt, etc.

Board doesn't mean a piece of wood, but a stiff form of paper substrate, like compressed cardboard. **Illustration board** is a stiff, coated board for markers, pencil, ink, etc., or for mounting finished design work.

Archival means it will last until the end of time, or at least two hundred years, whichever comes first.

Rag means cotton or linen fibers (as in cloth rags), as opposed to wood fibers (cellulose). Paper with a high rag content is more archival and doesn't disintegrate when wet. That's why paper money comes out of the washer and dryer just fine—it's made of 100 percent rag paper. Good stuff.

Tooth is the slight roughness on some papers that allows pencil, charcoal, etc., to grab hold of the paper and create a slight texture.

Prime: Some substrates need to be *primed* before you use them so the paint will adhere better. Prime a surface by painting it with gesso, either white, clear, or black. Also consider priming a substrate with absorbent ground (page 19 or 60).

Bond paper

You can use fine-grained white bond paper for sketches and layouts in pencil or marker. Bond paper is available in pads in sizes ranging from 9″ x 12″ to 19″ x 24″. We designers churn through reams of 8.5″ x 11″ bond on our desktop printers.

Everywhere I go, I carry 3″ x 5″ cards for "idea captures." My favorite cards are small, white, unruled, and are made of bond paper—card stock, to be exact. (Robin uses her iPhone's Notes pad, and those notes get synced to Mail on her Mac.)

Tracing paper

Tracing paper is thin, semi-transparent paper that you can place on top of an image and trace. It comes in pads and rolls of various sizes and weights.

Use *lightweight* tracing paper for creating thumbnails (small, quick idea sketches), as well as for tracing.

I prefer *heavyweight* tracing paper, also called **vellum.** It takes well to markers and Prismacolor pencils, and is durable enough to allow for erasing and the removal of marker color with an X-acto knife. Canson Vidalon 90 and 110 are a couple of my favorites.

Layout and visualizing paper

This is a translucent paper that tends to be more opaque than tracing paper, but more translucent than regular bond papers.

Its tooth makes it receptive to pencil, charcoal, and pastels. The best papers have a rag content which makes them strong and receptive to juicy markers.

There are layout and visualizing papers specifically created for markers that retain sharpness without bleeding through. My favorite brand is a pad of 9″ x 12″ Bienfang Graphics 360.

Printing paper

You can find printing papers (papers for use on a commercial printing press) in text and cover weight at art supply, craft, scrapbook stores, and online. Print shops and paper merchants can also provide sample sheets. When you create a comp (a comprehensive facsimile of the finished 2D project) for a client, the client gets a better idea of how the project will look when printed if you use the actual paper that the project will be printed onto.

Designers can acquire sample books of printing papers from paper manufacturers.

Metallic papers are thin, foil-laminated sheets and come with regular or peel-off backing. Use metallic foil papers when creating comps where you want to simulate foil stamping or for projects such as beverage labels.

Art paper

Art papers usually come as large, single sheets and range in price from $1.10 to more than $30. They are useful in creating spectacular collages and for integrating interesting textures and backgrounds into your work.

Art papers are easily scanned—just make sure you don't scan a copyrighted art paper. Some of the more pricey sheets are actually "works of art" and are copyrighted by the paper artist. Make sure you check the back of the sheet before you scan it and put it in your design work. Lawsuits are no fun.

Watercolor paper

The best watercolor papers have a high rag content.

Watercolor paper comes in **cold press** and **hot press:** Cold press has a textured surface; hot press has a smooth surface.

The heavier the paper, the less likely it is to buckle when you put water media on it. A good weight for most work is 140# (140 pound).

Fine quality papers such as Arches, Rives BFK, or Lana (from France) have very nice surfaces on which to work.

Canvas

Robin does not have a good relationship with watercolors so she prefers to use canvas from a canvas pad. She buys the 9" x 12" size so there's not a huge piece that looks intimidating, plus it fits on the scanner. And it doesn't wrinkle like watercolor paper. And she uses acrylics anyway.

You can also buy canvas in a roll or stretched onto wooden bars. You typically want to paint it first, called *priming* it, with something like white gesso (see page 17) to make sure the paint adheres well. Some canvas comes already primed and ready to use.

   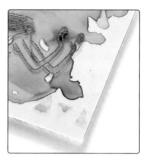 

Bristol board

Bristol board is a white sturdy paper, usually archival, that you can get in sheets or pads. It comes in thicknesses of 1- to 5-ply, which refers to how many layers of paper have been laminated together. You can use either side of the page.

The *vellum* Bristol is suitable for media that need some tooth to the surface. The *plate finish* is great for pen, ink, some pencil techniques, and spraying—any dry media that needs a smooth surface. A good quality Bristol such as Strathmore 400 to 500 is made with cotton fiber and will take repeated erasures without "feathering."

Masonite

Masonite, or **hardboard,** is cheap and durable and very stiff. Prime it with GAC 100 or 700 (page 18), and then gesso (page 17) to prevent the color from leaking into your paint.

Robin loves masonite because it's less intimidating to put paint and other stuff on it—it looks rough and cheap and much less snobby and judgmental than lovely and expensive watercolor paper. And you don't feel so badly if you have to throw it away.

Artist panels, artist boards

These hardboard panels or artist boards are primed with gesso and ready to paint. You can get them with a smooth surface, a canvas-textured surface, or a clay surface for scratchboard.

A "cradled" panel has a frame around it, as shown above; protect or paint the edge, and you have a substrate that is ready to hang when you've finished incorporating it into your digital project.

Plexiglass

An inexpensive sheet of plexiglass from the art or hobby store can be used as an inking plate for printmaking (see Part 6).

Or apply media to both sides to create art with a sense of depth. Try the opaque crackle medium mentioned on page 36—apply it to one side of the plexiglass, let it dry thoroughly, then paint it with watery acrylics or watercolor and let the paint seep into the cracks. On the other side, use a different technique that doesn't completely hide the seeped-in paint.

To cut the plexiglass, score it well on one side with a utility knife, then snap it over the edge of a sturdy table.

Chipboard

Chipboard is an inexpensive, rigid, gray/brownish board used for making mockups (3D facsimiles of the finished products) of packaging and models. It is available in variously sized sheets with thicknesses ranging from $\frac{1}{16}$ to $\frac{3}{16}$ inches. Because it comes in such a variety of sizes and is so cheap, designers can't get along without it.

That stiff board on the back of your note pad? That's chipboard.

A denser, higher quality version is called **book board** or **binder's board.**

Stuff to Put on your Surfaces

Tools and materials

- Palettes
- Brushes
- Watercolors
- Acrylic paints
- Gesso
- Mediums
- GAC mediums
- Gels
- Modeling or molding paste
- Mod Podge
- Absorbent Ground
- Digital Ground

Palettes

My palette is just a big, plastic rectangle with wells for colors and a top to cover it. Some **watercolor** artists use large, white butchers' trays. It's important to have a large area for mixing colors (I find the tiny palettes a little dysfunctional).

Watercolor paint left in the palette, even if it's been dry for ten years, will turn into usable paint again as soon as you add water. It's kind of magical. So just leave your palette to dry.

For **acrylic paints,** use disposable palettes and only pour into it what paint you need because once it's dry, acrylic paint turns into plastic.

Brushes

For **watercolor,** generally use natural hair brushes. For **acrylic,** buy the synthetic brushes. For India **ink** or painting with **resist/frisket,** get brushes for those purposes (ask in the store), then don't use them for any other media.

Carmen, who is an artist, uses good, expensive brushes and takes excellent care of them. Me, I'm not an artist, so I buy cheap brushes and treat them poorly. I keep a jar of water nearby and toss the brushes into the water until I've got time to clean them. It helps prevent me from getting too intimidated about "painting."

Darlene McElroy taught me to use slick paper plates (see page 11) as palettes for acrylic paints. Since the acrylics dry into plastic, you can reuse them without getting colors mixed up. And then the plates become art pieces! ~R

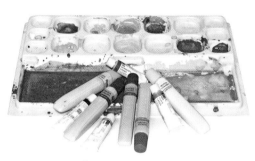

Watercolors

Watercolors are transparent, and they remain water soluble even after they've dried. This means you can take a wet brush to a finished watercolor painting and mess around in it even more, or put more watercolor on top of it and the two layers will mix together. It also means the only thing you can paint on are surfaces that don't repel water.

I personally prefer Winsor & Newton artist-grade watercolor paints, with a few Daniel Smith colors thrown in for good measure. But Grumbacher student-grade paints work just fine, especially for texture making. Find a good sale and stock up.

You will find that different colors cost more than others. That's because the mined pigments in Cobalt Blue are much rarer than, say, the earth materials used to make Burnt Umber. But you can't live without Cobalt Blue, so fork over that Visa card.

Acrylic paints

Acrylic paints are essentially opaque watercolors in a polymer base. You can water them down so they're less opaque (but don't add more than 30 percent water or the paint will not form a stable base), or thin them with glazing liquid, medium, or gel (as described on the following pages), which also makes them stay "open," or workable, for longer. Acrylics dry quickly, like in 10–15 minutes.

When dry, acrylic paints are impervious to water or any of the mediums or gels. Thus you can mix all these things together (acrylic paints and mediums and gels) in terrific ways, plus you can apply acrylic paint to a much wider variety of surfaces than you can watercolor.

Hard body acrylic: Fairly stiff, almost like frosting. Matte finish.

Soft body: Like heavy cream. Shows little or no brush marks. Dries to a satin finish.

Fluid: Very liquid paint, high pigment levels. Great for pouring and applying to fabric.

You can change the finish of any acrylic by using the appropriate gel or medium. For many projects that you plan to digitize, the cheap acrylics from craft or hobby stores (on the right in the photo above) will work just fine.

Gesso

Gesso is traditionally used to prime substrates (it originally contained rabbit-skin glue) to provide a surface to which oil paint will adhere better and to prevent any dirts or oils in the substrate from being lifted into the surface layer of paint as it dries. Modern acrylic gesso is another polymer medium so it plays really well with acrylic paints; prime just about any substrate with it.

If the look of your piece makes you unhappy, slather some gesso on it and start over.

Gesso is also great for adding texture—try using a palette knife or putty knife to apply it.

Mediums

"Medium" sounds like a generic term, but that's actually the name on the bottle or jar. Mediums are pourable.

The two kinds of mediums we work with in this book are **matte medium** (which gives, of course, a matte or non-glossy finish) and **polymer medium** (which gives a glossy finish). These mediums are more liquid than gels or pastes.

You'll use mediums to mix with acrylic paints to make them heavier or lighter, more transparent, to create texture on a page, or to keep the paint "open" longer so you can work with it (acrylics can dry so fast).

In all polymer products, the glossier the medium, the more transparent it is. A matte finish tends to be a bit translucent, especially if you layer it on thickly. That's not a bad thing, but keep it in mind as you choose products to work with.

GAC mediums

GAC mediums are the raw materials from which other acrylic mediums are created; they have the least amount of thickeners and other additives.

Each GAC medium can modify the characteristics and appearance of acrylic paints in a specific way, so read the labels. For instance, different GACs (they're numbered 100, 200, 900, etc.) can prime surfaces, stiffen fabric (allowing you to sculpt it) or stretched canvas (for painting ease), increase adhesion on non-porous surfaces, increase the hardness or the clarity of the paint, create a very glossy surface (great for glazing), mix with acrylic paint to make it go through the laundry, and more.

We don't use GAC mediums in the projects in this book, but you'll see them in the store so we wanted you to know what they are—hopefully you will start experimenting with them!

Gels

Basic gel comes in jars of soft, regular and hard; each version is available in matte, semi-gloss, and glossy finishes. They are actually acrylic paint without the pigment. Gels are *spreadable* (as opposed to mediums, which are *pourable*).

Use gels to create glazes (making acrylic paints transparent), texture, extend the paint, change the finish, transfer images, etc.

Soft glossy gel in particular is a great glue for paper collage.

Clear tar gel is a pourable gel, extremely glossy, and very fluid—drizzle it on your painted surface and it will make what is underneath shine.

Gels with inclusions, such as tiny glass beads or ground pumice, provide even more creative opportunities.

Modeling or molding paste

This is what we use to create amazing textures in Chapter 7; it's essentially a very heavy, opaque gel that's mixed with ground marble. It dries white (gels and mediums dry clear). It creates a fairly *slick* surface, which means paint might puddle.

Light molding paste has microscopic air bubbles instead of ground marble, so it's very light and fluffy. It creates a very *porous* surface so paint will absorb and bleed in interesting ways.

You can also use molding paste to extend the paint without adding transparency, as gels and mediums would, although the paint will be a little lighter in value.

Mod Podge

Mod Podge is the original decoupage medium. It's cheap, comes in many varieties, and can be used as a sealer, glue, or a finishing coat (with sanding).

Absorbent Ground

This was developed for a watercolor artist who wanted to paint on canvas. Apply it to any fairly heavy surface to make the surface respond almost like watercolor paper. You can apply several thin coats, letting it dry between each, building up a texture.

Digital Ground

Paint Digital Ground (white or clear) onto just about anything and then put that through your inkjet printer. This product lets you print onto tin foil, acrylic skins (paint you have poured onto a sheet of plastic and then peeled up), foil papers, and more. Paint on the Digital Ground, tape the surface to a piece of bond paper, and put it through an inexpensive printer. See an example on page 149.

Tips!

- **Buy at least** one container of matte or semi-gloss gel and one of matte medium and start using them in your handmade elements. You can only discover their properties and advantages as you work with them.

- All polymer products are also **adhesives,** so you can use any gel or medium to adhere papers and objects.

- Sometimes I want to merely **tint** or color a project without obscuring the texture or image already on the page. To do this, I add just a little acrylic paint to the medium or gel; I can then tint all or part of the page, tone it back, or cohere the elements on the page (or some of them) without obscuring any of the texture or images on it.

- Since I scan many of my pieces, I try to avoid the shiny surfaces that result from glossy media—I don't want to end up with **hot spots** on my images where the scanning lights cause glare. A matte surface doesn't create the reflection for a glare.

- But keep in mind that the glossier a medium is, the more **transparent** it will dry.

3 Transfer an Image to a Surface

Tools and materials

- Images printed from your computer, or from a type book, a book in the public domain, hand-drawn images, etc.
- Substrate: Bristol board, watercolor paper, scratch board, illustration board, canvas . . .
- Tracing paper
- #7 mechanical pencil with #2 lead (or any soft pencil)
- Graphite paper (optional)

If you are creating handmade illustrations of any sort, you often need to transfer your chosen images to other substrates, such as scratchboard or a rubber carving block.

The technique on the opposite page is quick and cheap, so it's great for images that are 100 percent of the size you want the final piece to be. But remember—you're a digital designer; once you have the final product in any size, you can scan and reproduce it as large as necessary.

To print onto tracing paper, tape the tracing paper onto a piece of printer paper; tape across the top and 2" down each side, then send it through the copier or printer.

To transfer an image to a large surface, try projecting it from your computer with a digital projector. Or, many libraries still have "opaque projectors" they might let you use—it's great old technology. If you need to transfer enlarged or reduced images often, go to Artograph.com and check out their line of art projectors (or lightboxes); you can get a small one for as little as $50.

Using graphite paper

1 First trace your letterforms or image carefully using a good quality tracing paper and a fine-point pen or dark pencil. Put drafting dots or masking tape at the corners to keep your tracing paper from slipping. If you need precise lines, use a lightbox, or tape your image and tracing paper to a window.

2 Once you've got your image on the tracing paper, put a sheet of graphite paper face down on your substrate (in this example, I'm transferring to a rubber carving block). Place your traced image on top and redraw over your tracing, checking to make sure you are pressing hard to transfer the image to your substrate.

Using a pencil

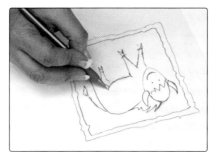

1 Draw or trace an image onto a piece of tracing paper or other lightweight paper. Make sure it's nice and dark.

3 Turn your tracing back over and carefully position the *scribbly pencil* side onto your chosen substrate. Use drafting dots, masking tape, or skin tape (from the drug store) to fasten it firmly to the substrate.

4 Retrace your image using firm, but not harsh, pressure.

2 Turn your tracing over and scribble all across the *back* side of the paper with your soft pencil. Cover it well.

5 Peel back a corner of the tracing paper to make sure your image is transferring neatly.

> **Tip!** *You can also iron images onto some substrates!*
>
> *If your image is from a photocopy machine or a laser printer (not an inkjet printer), you can transfer it onto wood, cloth, glass, and other surfaces with heat from a household iron or a heat transfer tool (shown left) that you can buy in craft stores.* **~R**

4 Heat, Cut, Score, Perforate

Tools and Materials

- Metal rulers: 18″ cork-backed ruler, deckle-edged ruler, centering rule
- For scoring, screen spline tool (for fixing window screens) and pizza cutter
- Carl rotary trimmer with a cutting blade, scoring blade, and deckle blade
- Martha Stewart's circle cutter
- Scoring styluses with different tips
- Burnishing tools with tips that can be used for scoring
- Bone folder
- X-acto knife with #11 blades
- Swivel knife
- Paper scissors
- Acrylic rolling burnisher
- Utility knife
- Box cutter with extra blades
- Schadler rulers

Many of my tools pictured above are more than thirty years old. Good tools that are carefully taken care of will last you a lifetime. I believe in high-quality tools because they make it so much easier to work on projects. Remember, in graphic design, time is money (which is why I swear by my Macintosh computer—I can depend on it!). Consequently, I buy the best tools and materials I can afford and then make an effort to take good care of them. I clean them and keep them in a case or plastic bin where they are protected and I can find them.

You don't need *all* these tools shown here to get started, of course! We just want you to know what they are so when you need one, you'll know what it looks like. And remember, once you invest in any tool, all kinds of ways to use it show up!

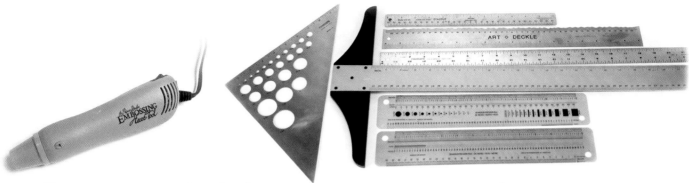

Heat gun

Yes, this looks like a hair dryer, but it puts out a lot more heat and much less wind (do *not* use it on your hair—it will burn it off!). You'll find a heat gun handy for all sorts of artsy-crafty things, and you can't emboss the powders in Chapter 36 without it.

Self-healing mat

Please see page 127 for the importance of owning a self-healing cutting mat to use with all these cutting devices!

Metal rulers

Nothing beats an 18″ **cork-backed ruler** when you need to cut things with an X-acto knife. The cork helps keep your ruler from slipping when you cut (if you use plastic rulers with your sharp knives, it is very easy to cut a chunk right out of the ruler and thus render it virtually worthless). The cork raises the ruler edge off the sensitive paper, which protects our sensitive digital output and, if you're inking, prevents the ink from smearing.

I use a **centering rule** to help mount presentations or certain collage elements because it gives me an instant center mark.

A **deckle-edged ruler** is great for creating rough edges—lay it down on a piece of paper and pull up the paper, pulling *toward* the ruler, so it tears along the rough edge.

Measuring tools

The **Schadler rulers** are wonderful—if you're measuring down to $\frac{1}{64}$th of an inch, these are the rulers you want because they actually have the 64ths of an inch marked and counted. These rulers are printed on a very stable material and have every measuring scale you can think of. They are totally flexible—you can measure around something like a beverage can. The rulers are very thin, so you don't get your measurements off by the thickness of your ruler. They aren't cheap (about $30 for the set of two), but they are just perfect for exact measurements.

When putting together mockups, I use **metal rulers** because they are impervious to knife cuts—it's too easy to have that knife slip and cut your expensive Schadler rulers!

A strip of **scrap paper and a pencil** can work so well for measuring if you are trying to find center points or divide a specific width into something like sixths. Just fold your strip of paper into the appropriate number of sections. Open up and your folds are your marks. *Voilà!* No math!

Cutting tools

I carry a hot pink **X-acto knife** in my purse (everything in my purse is hot pink). I just never know when I might be required to whip together a comp at a moment's notice and I don't want to be unprepared or under accessorized.

An observation I have made over the years is that designers tend to be frugal with art supplies and totally indulgent with technology. They absolutely have to have the latest, greatest computer and software, but refuse to spring for extra blades for their cutting tools. Consequently, they mow through several expensive sheets of photo paper or present a less-than-stellar comp because they won't take the time to buy or change their X-acto knife blades.

Another issue with cutting tools: Don't send a girl out to do a woman's job. That is, don't try to cut heavy chipboard with a dainty #11 knife blade—for heaven's sake, go steal your sweetheart's drywall knife, or better yet, buy yourself one. However, don't use that same **hefty utility knife** to cut delicate sheets of vellum—you'll end up with crumpled, ragged edges.

And change your blades often.

When I saw Carmen's scissor collection, I was so envious I immediately went out and bought myself a set. I used them to trim colored construction paper to make the edges you see on every left-hand page in this book.

~R

There are a couple of specialty cutting tools worth considering. One is a **circle cutter** (shown to the left) which is useful for cutting round packaging labels or stickers. Martha Stewart and Making Memories are both excellent brands.

Another tool that I pull out from time to time is a **swivel knife** (shown to the right). This is a craft knife (like an X-acto knife; in fact, X-acto makes a swivel blade) that rotates and lets you cut curves smoothly (if you have old French curves, use those as templates!).

And I love my **fancy scissors** that have decorative blades for creating distinctive edges on papers.

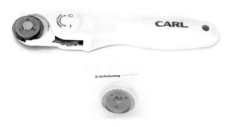

Perforating tools

When it comes to creating great comps (physical, 2D facsimiles to show the client what the finished piece will look like), it's all about the details. For instance, if you are creating a brochure and it has a tear-off card to send back, why not actually put in the *perfs* (the perforations)?

A company named Carl makes a wonderful rotary cutter, as shown above. You can change the blades very easily to create different decorative edges, perforate paper, trim paper, or score paper.

I'm saving my pennies and one of these days I'm going to spring for the $300 deluxe model that cuts thirty sheets of paper perfectly at one time.

Scoring and folding tools

Scoring tools help make folds nice and crisp. You can collect quite a nice fistful of these useful tools, or you can open your kitchen drawer and pull out your **pizza cutter.**

I use quite a few tools for scoring because I like to match the tip to the type of paper stock I'm using. For instance, if I'm folding a delicate vellum, I might use the very tiny ball tip of an **embossing tool** (far right images in photo above). If I'm assembling a large signage mockup with heavy chipboard, I might use a **burnisher** that has a ball about the size of a pea on one end.

To score for easy folding, use a ruler and run the scoring tool along the outside fold line. This bends the fibers just enough to create a crisp fold. Once folded, burnish the folded edge on the outside with a **bone folder** (see top, right).

Burnishing tools

In this photo there is, left to right, a **brayer,** a **bone folder,** and a **baren.** You could also use the back of a large metal spoon—or a small one, depending on the need. And it's good to have an official **burnisher** tool as shown in the center photo (the three tools with colored handles).

A couple of burnishing tools can rub down those edges that want to pop up on the collage you need to scan, fasten your digital output to your packaging substrate, and help transfer the ink from your linocut or monoprint to the paper.

Burnishing tools will give you your life back—heaven knows we spend half of our lives fixing stuff in Photoshop. We don't need to spend more time touching up our images if we can avoid it with good crafts-manship to begin with.

5 Adhesives—Glue it Down

Tools and materials

- Xyron gadgets
- Hot glue gun
- StudioTac dry adhesive
- Rubber cement and pickup
- Easy-Tack Repositionable Adhesive
- Spray Mount Artist's Adhesive
- Super 77 Multipurpose Adhesive
- UHU Tac plastic adhesive
- Yes! Paste
- Yasutomo Nori
- Bookbinder's glue
- Aleene's Tacky Glue
- Amazing Goop contact adhesive, Amazing E-6000, and other contact cements
- Goo Gone, 3M Adhesive Remover Pen, and Gunk & Goo Remover Towelettes

Adhesives. The very word causes many digital designers to have a full-blown panic attack. The very thought of getting anything sticky near their precious digital output is enough to send them over the edge, and thus their clients are handed floppy photopaper prints or are required to squint at Illustrator files on a 13" laptop instead of being handed a perfect comp. These same designers wonder why it is so hard to sell their ideas.

Designers need to buck up, take a deep breath, face their fears: Get out that X-acto knife, some appropriate adhesives, and mount your presentations, build a beautifully crafted mockup, or put together an original illustration. Holding a well-crafted mockup or comp makes the project more "real" for many clients and helps sell the concept.

Xyron gadgets

This product is a favorite with the scrapbooking crowd because it creates stickers, labels, magnets, or laminates any digital output or sheet of decorative paper. It's a little roller gadget that spreads a thin layer of sticky adhesive from a transfer roll onto your material.

I like it because you don't have to deal with spray adhesive mist all over everything and causing a mess. The Xyron adhesive goes on very thin so you don't get bumps showing through your digital presentation papers, like you can with spray adhesive when it splatters, or glue if you don't spread it smoothly.

The Xyron isn't cheap. The unit that supports 8.5″ x 11″ paper costs $120, and each cartridge costs $35. But I think it's worth the price because I don't mess up my digital prints, breathe spray adhesives, or discover my poor poodle, Zinnie, with dust bunnies sticking to her ears.

Hot glue gun

We have the crafters and carpenters to thank for this useful tool. You can purchase this little heater in all colors, sizes, and temperatures. I often use it for creating found-object illustrations. I like the hotter temps because the glues bind better and aren't so stringy; however, I have burnt a finger or two putting together some fantastic piece, so you do have to be careful. Nonetheless, when you are perching a little something or other in a precarious position and you need it glued solid NOW, there is nothing better than a hot glue gun to get the job done.

But don't use it with polymer clay (see page 30 for adhesives to use with baked clay).

StudioTac dry adhesive

This wonderful product should be in every designer's tool box—it's portable, tidy, and very easy to use. Basically, StudioTac consists of carrier sheets with tiny dots of adhesive temporarily clinging to them. With a burnishing tool, you can transfer the adhesive to papers and other light, fairly flat materials that need to be glued. It works particularly well for those small pieces you want to add to your collage.

StudioTac is available in permanent or low-tack versions. The low-tack is great when you want to do something like mount a piece on a presentation board, but later need to transfer the same piece to a portfolio page. Easy as can be.

> **Tip!** Any polymer gel or medium (see Chapter 1), including acrylic paint, is also a glue that becomes water-insoluble when dry!

Rubber cement and pickup

I have used gallons of rubber cement in my life. It was the adhesive of choice next to hot wax when we had to create "boards" back in the day before computers took over the design industry. I don't use it now because I have found so many other products that aren't as smelly. However, there are a couple of great qualities to rubber cement—it gives you a moment to wiggle things in place before it dries, and it doesn't buckle the paper.

You must invest in the thinner as well as the cement. The chemicals in rubber cement dissipate quickly, leaving behind a thick rubbery blob that is impossible to spread in a thin, even coat. Keep a bottle of solvent thinner close at hand to mix in when things start to get a little stretchy.

And get or make a **rubber cement pickup** (shown above, and see page 99) to clean up any excess that oozes out.

Easy-Tack Repositionable Adhesive

This is a repositionable, low-tack spray adhesive by Krylon. Use this when you want a temporary bond.

I use Easy-Tack for pieces mounted in my portfolio. I also use it when screen printing to keep things in register.

"Tack" refers to how sticky something is.

Spray Mount Artist's Adhesive

This spray adhesive is less tacky than Super 77. Spray Mount should work fine for most of your regular paper-mounting tasks.

To create a *very* tight bond, spray both of the surfaces that you wish to glue together, let them dry, and then put them together. You need to put them together *perfectly* the very first time because there is no forgiveness—this double bond sticks tighter than a strong magnet.

Super 77 Multipurpose Adhesive

This is the spray adhesive you'd use to fasten your carpet to the floor—industrial grade. It's the one to use when you never want to separate two pieces from each other ever again.

Make sure you keep the nozzle clean: When you are done with your gluing activities, tip the can upside down and give two squirts into a paper towel.

UHU Tac plastic adhesive

Remember when we used to put posters of our favorite rock 'n' roll stars on our walls? We called the white sticky stuff "poster putty." Well, UHU Tac is just such a product—a temporary adhesive that you can use to put a collage or found-object illustration together, without making a commitment. And as we are all too aware, our beloved clients tend to be a little phobic around commitments.

Yes! Paste

This is one of the most simple of adhesives and has been a favorite of collage artists for years. It is so unobtrusive if applied properly; it won't yellow or disintegrate, and it adheres perfectly.

But Yes! Paste isn't terribly easy to apply. You need scrap paper and a squeegee-type tool (a little rectangle of old mat board, a plastic spackle tool, or a putty knife from the hardware store) to apply the paste. Brushes don't work well with Yes! Paste because the bristle marks show through on thinner papers.

Make sure you keep the container closed tightly between uses because once it is even slightly dried out, it becomes lumpy and nearly impossible to spread smoothly.

I just wish we could purchase smaller containers of this wonderful product. My students blanch at paying about $15 for a jar, especially since it dries out so quickly.

Yasutomo Nori

This is a good alternative to Yes! Paste because it comes in a smaller container, is a little more liquid-like, and costs next to nothing. I personally use Yes! Paste because I don't like the juiciness of Nori, but nonetheless, Nori is a very simple and effective adhesive—perfect for collage. It's particularly great with delicate papers.

Bookbinder's glue

Polyvinyl acetate (PVA) is one of the strongest archival "white" glues available to the designer. This is the adhesive we use when we want something to be used over and over and still hold together, such as books. I also use it for my larger packaging mockups and pop-ups if I need a particularly strong bond.

PVA doesn't dry instantly, and it glues tight. In the case of packaging, use clothes pins to clamp your edges together and allow them to dry for several hours. In the case of books, make sure no glue oozes out because you don't want to glue your books shut.

Aleene's Tacky Glue

This is another favorite white glue—strong and archival. It tends to be thicker than book binder's glue and takes a little less time to dry.

I personally prefer the more liquid, smoother application of PVA. Nonetheless, Tacky Glue is a great product if applied carefully or if you're in a hurry for things to bond. Apply it with a squeegee to avoid lumps and bumps.

Aleene's has a variety of products for all sorts of gluing projects.

Amazing Goop contact adhesive, Amazing E-6000, and other contact cements

These are the adhesives I use with my clay sculpture and assemblage. They are industrial strength glues that have some give to them (like silicone) and they dry very quickly.

When you glue rigid, breakable elements like baked polymer clays, you need to have some flex between the pieces; otherwise they'll shatter if you put any pressure on them. Amazing E-6000, Amazing Goop, and other contact cements dry kind of spongey, which allows some shifting without breakage, whereas hot glue from a glue gun or Instant Krazy Glue are brittle and have no give.

Use E-6000 or Amazing Goop when building clay sculptures or when applying 3D elements to something like assemblage on canvas.

Goo Gone, 3M Adhesive Remover Pen, and Gunk & Goo Remover Towelettes

These are useful products for getting the sticky residue off your fingers, products, edges, and tools.

I use Goo Gone for removing wine-label residue when I want to make a mockup on an unopened bottle.

However, if you've made a real gluing mess, you might as well start over because these products can cause more residual stains than the adhesive used in the first place. They are basically for minor cleanups, not ultimate salvation.

PART 2

Texture your Surface

One contribution of handmade design is texture. I love texture. I love the tactile feel of papers and walls and stones and sand and fabric and pudding and animals and sculpture. And I enjoy visual texture. Texture gives two-dimensional design an engaging perceptible appeal that draws the audience into the piece. It's the quickest and easiest way to add a human touch to your digital design.

I encourage you to read about, experiment with, take notes on, and create your own handmade textures. Then scan these into your computer and use them in your graphic design work. Or perhaps collage various hand-textured items together before you scan the whole piece. It's very satisfying to get your hands dirty this way!

Textures

Background surfaces that have some texture add depth and richness to digital work.

6 Crackle the Surface

Want that aged look of crackled paint? It only takes a few minutes to create and can give your piece maturity.

See pages 34–37.

8 Create a Patina

A patina is an acquired change in the appearance of a surface, usually produced by age or weather. You can fake the process for a project.

See pages 42–45.

7 Texturize with Modeling Paste

Modeling pastes and gel mediums are basically acrylic paints without the pigments. Apply them to a variety of surfaces and then comb, scratch, swirl, or brush other elements into the paste to create a variety of textural effects.

See pages 38–41.

9 Peel the Paint

The look of peeled paint can add a sense of history to a modern piece.

See pages 46–49.

10 Rub and Rag

Darker paint rubbed into the more textural areas of a piece further enhances the tactile appeal.

See pages 50–55.

This half-sheet flyer is just fine without a handmade texture.

But using the texture adds not only a little extra visual richness, but an extra touch of the human.

11 Alcohol Inks

On non-porous surfaces, create rich, mottled textures with alcohol inks. Not even the artistically challenged can go wrong with this medium.

See pages 56–59.

12 Absorbent Ground and Washi Paper

Use Japanese papers and gel media to create texture you can touch.

See pages 60–65.

13 Monoprints

Create unique and vivid textures by using ink and glass together.

See pages 66–69.

14 Bubble Texture

Now you have a grown-up excuse to play with bubbles—you need that texture for a design project!

See pages 70–71.

6 Crackle the Surface

Tools and materials

- Acrylic paint in two contrasting colors
- Acrylic paint brush
- *Transparent* liquid crackle medium
- Heavy substrate such as 300 lb. watercolor paper, Bristol board, canvas, masonite, etc.

- Alternative method: Elmer's Glue-All and acrylic paints and brushes; see page 36

You can simulate the look of aging wood or raku (crackled) ceramic surfaces quite easily with a variety of crackle mediums. Some give fine eggshell lines that are very subtle; others make your texture look like shredded barn wood. I've tried all sorts of products and had fairly decent—and sometimes stunning— results with all of them. It just depends on how the materials dry.

The basic process is that two wet mediums with different drying times are layered on top of each other, and the result is a cracked surface. You can buy the crackle medium at art, craft, and some hardware stores. Each brand has its own set of directions, so be sure to read and follow them to the letter. You may want to create practice samples before committing to one.

Transparent crackle

This technique uses a transparent liquid for crackling. If you want a relatively smooth crackly texture, make sure you paint in the same direction each time, using long strokes. The thicker you paint it on, the larger the cracks. The instructions below are specifically for the brand I'm using, Village Folk Art. Be sure to read and follow the directions for the particular brand that you buy!

1 With acrylic paint, paint an area on your chosen substrate. Let it dry completely.

2 Paint over your first color with your chosen crackle medium.

   Let the medium dry.

3 Paint over the crackle medium with your *contrasting* color of acrylic paint.

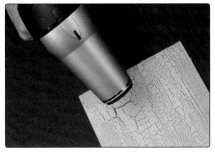

4 Let it air dry, or use a blow dryer. The cracks will appear before your eyes.

Kaitlin Glass used a crackle texture to add visual interest on this menu cover.

Opaque crackle paste

The medium labeled "Crackle Paste" is a thick, *opaque* material that creates deep, fissure-like cracks as it dries. You can layer it on up to an inch thick. Like the acrylic modeling pastes on pages 38–41, you can paint over it after it dries (which might take three days if it's thick!). You can also tint the paste with acrylic paints before you spread it on, or paint it afterwards.

Since this is a heavy-body medium, use a rigid support. It's a bit fragile when it dries, so give it a coat or two of polymer medium to protect it.

Transparent crackle with Elmer's Glue-All

Use household Elmer's Glue-All (basic white glue) as a crackle medium. It might not be as elegant, but it creates interesting textures. The thicker the glue and the less paint, the wider the cracks. Try it over a page of text from an old book or magazine and some of the text will show through. Stroke the paint in different directions to get a variety of crackly textures.

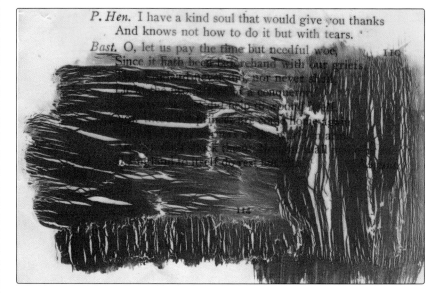

1 Pour on some Elmer's glue and paint it around on your page.

2 Before the glue dries, dip your brush in acrylic paint and wipe it into the glue. The less paint, the more of the under-page that you'll see. If you brush in different directions, you'll get different patterns of cracks.

   If your under-page has text on it, stroke your paint in the direction of the text so it will show through the cracks a bit.

3 Be patient and let it dry. The cracks will appear. You can use a heat gun or a hair dryer if you're impatient.

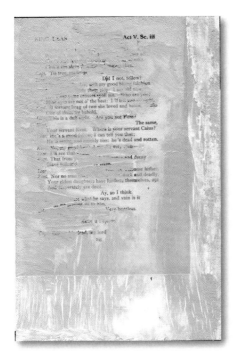

I tore out a page from an old, destroyed Shakespeare book and glued it onto a small sheet of canvas from a canvas pad. I used inexpensive Mod Podge to glue the page to the canvas, and painted Mod Podge over the paper to seal it (you could, of course, use your matte medium, polymer medium, or any gel).

When dry, I used Elmer's glue and acrylic paint to create a cracked, tortured background. I then made a simple collage on this page and used it as the basis for a program cover.

~R

7 Texturize with Modeling Paste

Tools and materials

- Heavy substrate like canvas, Bristol board, 300 lb. watercolor paper
- Modeling medium, modeling paste (also called molding paste), texture gel medium, or even spackling paste (spackle) that you might have in your garage
- Palette knife
- Squeegee tool for spreading medium
- Sticks, combs, forks, cake decorating tools . . .

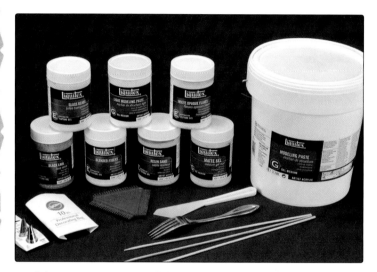

Modeling pastes come in different weights and have different application requirements depending on the specific one used. The consistency of some is that of frosting; others are more like heavy cream or gel.

You can apply these pastes to a variety of surfaces—canvas, Bristol board, illustration board, heavy watercolor papers, masonite—just about anything that has a hefty substance.

Once a paste is spread on the chosen surface but before it is dry, it's easy to comb, scratch, swirl, or brush other elements into it to create a variety of textural effects. When it's dry, you can paint it, top it with a metallic surface (see Chapter 8), spray it, rub color into it, sand it, carve it, and more.

About modeling or molding pastes

Modeling pastes are *opaque*. Feel free to add acrylic paint to the paste to tint it a nice pastel.

If your surface is not very rigid, ***light* modeling paste** works better than the ***regular* or *heavy* modeling paste.** Regular modeling pastes have a tendency to crack if the substrate is too flimsy or the paste is applied heavily. (Sometimes this can turn out to be a great effect, so experiment!)

Light modeling pastes and spackle are *absorbent* so water-based media (watercolors or acrylic paints) are going to get absorbed into the texture. **Heavy modeling paste is *non-absorbent*** so the paint will sit on top. I'll show you how to work with the pastes on the next page.

Other *non-absorbent* media you can use are heavy-body acrylic paints, acrylic gessos, or hard gels, all of which come in either opaque or transparent (see Chapter 2 for details on those products).

Some of these pastes and gels come with **inclusions** such as glass beads, fibers, ground lava rock, sand, etc., built into the goo. The inclusions can react with the next layer of paint in interesting ways. It's easy to add your own inclusions, such as sand or dried autumn leaves, as long as the items you add are really dry (you don't want rotting illustrations).

You can also use some of the more liquid products (such as matte medium or clear tar gel; again, see Chapter 2) to create texture—drip, spatter, and smear them onto the substrate for gestural effects.

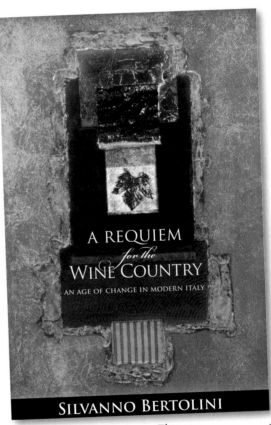

This piece uses several layers of modeling paste textures.

Modeling or molding paste

Remember that flexible or light modeling pastes work better on lightweight substrates. If you use the heavier modeling medium or paste, use canvas, artist panels, or other rigid substrates.

TIP! *Make sure you close up your jars tightly. This material dries quite quickly and isn't cheap.*

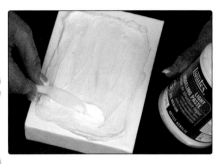

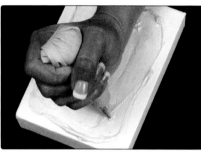

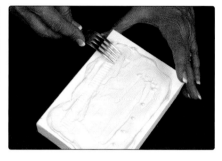

1 Open the jar. With a pallet knife, scoop out a hefty glob of modeling paste (or other medium that you have on hand).

2 Spread the paste around with a palette knife or squeegee until you get the look and feel you want. It's kind of like spreading frosting or spackle. I've even used my cake decorating tools (as shown above) to create dots or lines on the surface. (Buy a set specifically for your art work; don't use your cake set for polymer media. Or use an envelope or baggie with a cut corner, or wax paper rolled into a cone.)

3 Scratch in the paste with sticks, forks, combs, garden tools, etc. Because the modeling paste is polymer-based, it acts as an adhesive so you can stick things in it and they'll stay. Experiment with the possibilities.

Your textured piece serves as a base for other techniques. Paint it, carve it, sand it, etc. To the left, you can see that I applied a metallic color to this piece and then rubbed dark paint in the crevices to emphasize the texture (see Chapter 10).

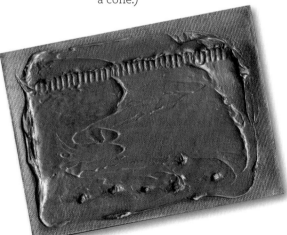

Try this!

Here are several other techniques to use with modeling paste.

- Spread the medium over a painted surface. Using any kind of sharp tool or old hotel card key or credit card, scratch back through the modeling paste to expose that painted surface.

- Spread a thin layer of modeling paste onto a surface. Then push a stencil, a simple stamp, or textured wallpaper into it.

- Lay a stencil on top of a painted surface (or attach it lightly with Easy-Tack; see page 28). Gently use a palette knife or putty knife to smear modeling paste into the open stencil areas.

- Don't limit yourself to texturizing flat surfaces! You can spread modeling paste on all kinds of things and add them to your digital work.

For this postcard announcing Janice's gallery opening, I created a background with modeling paste to correspond with the ancient pottery look of her painted gourds. I had earlier created the dry-brush letter G (a dry brush dipped in watercolor, painted onto dry paper) for the gallery. The G is black, but after I placed it on the page in InDesign, I gave it the "Overlay" effect from the Effects palette.

These jars have a layer of modeling paste and several layers of rubbed-and-ragged paint to make them more interesting.

41

8 Create a Patina

Tools and materials

- Piece of metal or a metal-leafed surface *or...*
- Topper product in metallic effect desired: copper, iron, bronze

Also:

- Patina medium in metallic aging effect desired: copper, iron, bronze
- Heavy substrate such as Bristol or illustration board, canvas, heavy watercolor paper, masonite, artist panel
- Paint brushes: one brush for acrylic paint and one old, scruffy brush

A patina is that lovely look that many things acquire with age—the greenish film on oxidized copper or bronze, the rich sheen of old, polished wood, or the beauty of older women (say Robin and Carmen).

You don't have to wait years for a patina that you might need for a particular project, though. You can apply a patina to an actual piece of metal as long as the metal hasn't been sealed (if you think it has a seal, remove it with lacquer thinner).

Or create your own fake metal surface using a metallic "topper" (as explained on the opposite page) such as those made by Sophisticated Finishes or Modern Optics Metallic Surfacers, or use a surface that you have covered with metal leafing.

Apply the patina medium

You can purchase thin sheets of art metals from an art supply store or a craft store. You might want to emboss a design into the metal with a stylus or any pointy object before you apply a patina.

If you're creating a fake metal surface, use a more rigid surface such as Bristol or illustration boards, heavy watercolor papers, or even canvas so you won't end up with your project all buckled from the wet media.

After the base has dried, the patina coat of acid discolors the surface and gives the unpredictable effects of metal left to the elements. You must wait several hours or overnight for the patina coat to work its magic, so don't hold your breath. *Test it before you apply a patina to your original piece!*

To test the patina effect for a project, I used this little piece of copper that I had embossed with an inexpensive embossing tool. ~R

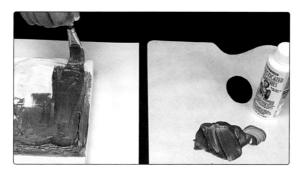

Step 1 creates a fake metallic surface. If you are using an actual metallic surface or metal-leafed surface, skip to Step 2.

1   To create a fake metallic surface on another substrate, you need a product called a "topper" or "metallic surfacer," which you can find in an art supply or craft store. Paint an area with the topper and let it dry. If you're as impatient as I am, use a craft dryer or hair dryer to speed up the drying.

In this example I'm using a texture that I had previously created with acrylic paste, as described in Chapter 7. I'm covering it with a metal leafing product called Sophisticated Finishes Gold Metallic Surfacer.

—continued

2 After your metal is clean or your topper is dry, paint on the patina product. Shake the bottle hard—the acid crystals sometimes settle out and you need to get everything mixed up thoroughly.

Above, I'm applying the patina to the canvas that I previously covered with gold metal leaf.

3 Paint the patina product over the entire surface or just the portion you want to discolor.

At first the result may seem rather disappointing. Let it sit overnight for the patina to take effect. Part of the charm of this product is its unpredictability, so just let it be.

A bit of patina in this watercolor and collage gives it an organic edge.

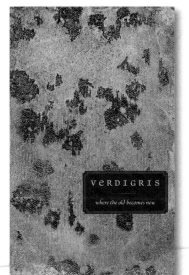

VERDIGRIS

where the old becomes new

Strips taken from this cover texture become dividers inside this small, fold-out brochure.

ABOUT US

Quia voluptatus inci dolupti usdam, simi, as ditiatur auda sum, omnist volupta cusae laut quamus aut quam vero et, con re, simus nihitat laudios molupta sequo iunt is pliti cuptum in nobis ut vere ello beatiur, omnimaximust liquae vel es denis sandis ario officab il idescidipsus doluptasi doluptatur sectatem laboritis sequossimint alis aut.

· Sed quo maximin nus.

· Gendant ullabor ernatur repudam, aut il ea dolor reris natures dendis necaecu lparibus pro maio.

· Eces ut dolupid estiatis mos eum res nest aliberrovide voloreperum voluptatum eos dolum qui ut assum.

FURNITURE

Aut quam vero et, con re, simus quia voluptatus inci dolupti usdam, simi, as ditiatur auda sum, omnist volupta cusae laut quamus aut quam verro et. Con re simus nihitat laudios molupta sequo iunt is pliti cuptum in nobis ut vere ello beatiur, omni maximust. Liquae vel es denis sandis ario officab il idescidipsus doluptasi.

· Dolor reris natures dendis necaecu lparibus pro.

· Maximin nusendant ullabor ernatur repudam, aut il ea dolor.

· Estiatis mos eum res nest. Aliberrovide voloreperum voluptatum.

LIGHTING

Voluptatus inci dolupti usdam, simi, as ditiatur auda sum, omnist volupta cusae laut quamus aut quam verro et. Con re simus nihitat laudios molupta sequo iunt is pliti cuptum in nobis ut vere ello. Beatiur, omnimaximust liquae vel es denis.

· Quo maximin nussed.

· Maio pendant ullabor ernatur repudam, aut il ea dolor reris natures dendis necaecu lparibus pro. Eces ut dolupid estiatis mos eum res nest aliberrovide voloreperum voluptatum eos dolum qui ut assum.

ART

Nobis wuia voluptatus inci dolupti usdam, simi, as ditiatur auda sum, omnist volupta cusae laut quamus aut quam verro et, con re, simus nihitat laudios molupta sequo iunt is pliti cuptum in ut vere ello beatiur, omnimaximust liquae vel es denis sandis ario officab il idescidipsus doluptasi doluptatur sectatem laboritis sequossimint alis aut. Sed quo maximin nus es denis sandis ario officab.

· Gendant ullabor ernatur repudam, aut il ea dolor reris natures dendis necaecu lparibus pro maio.

· Eces ut dolupid estiatis mos eum res nest aliberrovide voloreperum voluptatum eos dolum qui ut assum.

CLOTHES

Molupta buia voluptatus inci dolupti usdam, simi, as ditiatur auda sum, omnist volupta cusae laut quamus aut quam verro et, con re, simus. Nihitat laudios molupta sequo iunt is pliti cuptum in nobis ut vere ello beatiur, omnimaximust liquae vel es denis sandis ario officab il idescidipsus doluptasi doluptatur sectatem laboritis sequossimint alis aut.

· Eces ut dolupid estiatis mos eum res nest aliberrovide voloreperum voluptatum eos dolum qui ut assum.

SHOES

Simi as ditiatur auda sum, omnist volupta cusae laut quamus aut quam verro et, con re, simus. Nihitat laudios molupta sequo iunt is pliti cuptum in nobis ut vere ello beatiur, omni maximust liquae vel es denis. Sandis ario officab il ides cidipsus dolup tasi dolup tatur sectatem laboritis sequossimint.

· Sequossimint alis aut nus.

· Ernatur repudam, aut il ea dolor reris natures dendis lparibus pro necaecu.

· Dolupid estiatis mos eum res nest.

BOOKS

Laut quamus aut quam laudios. Molupta sequo vere ello beatiur, or sandis ario officab il sectat em laboritis

· Omni mai Sedera e

· Qemat natures

· Volupta eum r eos m

the patina of marriage

a discussion of the weathering process

documentary and talk

9 Peel the Paint

Tools and materials

- A rigid substrate such as canvas, illustration board, or artist panel, on which is mounted a painting, photograph, image, texture, or illustration
- Matte medium
- Petroleum jelly
- Acrylic paint
- Paint brush
- Paper towels
- Soap and water or baby wipes

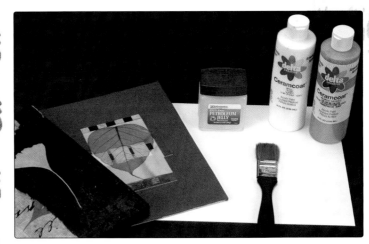

*I didn't have petroleum jelly on hand so I tried Vick's VapoRub and created the piece above. It worked great.
~R*

This technique gives the effect of old peeling paint. Use an image that you either painted or decoupaged* onto a rigid surface such as canvas, Bristol, or illustration board. By using layers of simple petroleum jelly and acrylic paint, it's easy to give your image that ancient or grungy look that can be just the effect you are looking for.

*To decoupage, simply get a jar of gel (see page 18) from an art supply store or Mod Podge from a hobby store. Use it to glue the images onto the substrate, then paint several coats of the gel on top of the image to seal it (let it dry between coats).

Peeling paint

An important step in this technique is to create a resilient background that won't fall apart when it's wet or when you're rubbing it. You *can* use a paper substrate such as Bristol, but it will be safer for your project to use something a little sturdier. In this example I'm using a canvas board.

1   Spray-paint a background color on your substrate, or paint a coat of acrylic on it.

2   **Important:** Since this piece is going to be washed off with water, protect the background you just created by painting it with a coat of polymer medium (which is glossy), matte medium (which is matte), gel (various finishes), or Mod Podge (all kinds of finishes). Let it dry completely.

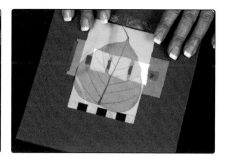

3   Take an image, photograph, or digital print of a collage you made (by hand, of course) and use your preferred medium to glue the image to the substrate.

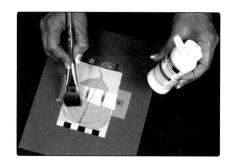

4   Seal the entire piece with the medium. If you're in a hurry, use a heat gun to speed up the drying process.

Emily Roberts designed this magazine page with a collage that uses a peeled paint background.

—continued

5   When the piece is bone dry, take petroleum jelly and spread it *on the areas of the surface that you want to have peek through the peeling paint*. Put the jelly on with your fingers, and put it on thick, but make sure you don't have peaks or globs.

6   Once you have jellied the surface, paint the entire piece with acrylic paint that you've thinned with water to the consistency of chocolate syrup. Paint lightly—don't mix the petroleum jelly into the paint.

Leave the painting to dry on its own away from anything warm; you don't want the petroleum jelly to turn to liquid and mix with the drying paint.

8   After you have removed most of the paint and jelly this way, gently wash the canvas with a little dish detergent and water in a sink. Rub very carefully so you don't damage the surface.

7   Once all the paint is dry, take a paper towel and gently rub off the paint and petroleum jelly—the paint will lift away from the background with the jelly. If some paint gets stuck, scratch it off with a fingernail.

Note! *If you used a paper substrate such as Bristol board, don't wash off the piece under the faucet! You can use baby wipes to get the jelly and paint off the surface, and you'll just have to live with the slightly oily surface it creates.*

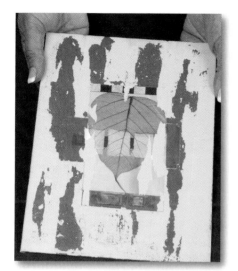

9 As an added protection to the piece and to make sure nothing sticks to your scanner glass, brush on a final coat of medium or gel as a sealer. Let it dry thoroughly.

In this poster, the peeling paint adds a sense of uncovering secrets that have been hidden.

10 Rub and Rag the Paint

Tools and materials

- Any painted piece that has some texture in it, such as one with modeling paste (see Chapter 7), masking tape (see Chapter 25), or a collage
- Acrylic paints
- Paint brush
- Palette of some sort
- Paper towels or cotton rags

When paint gets rubbed into the crevices of a textured piece, it creates beautiful depth and richness. You'll find this technique to be one of the most often used in your repertoire. Combine it with any technique that creates even the slightest texture on the page, and even try it on a smoothly painted background—rub in some paint and rub most of it off, leaving just a mottled layer of complexity.

Tip! *Also try sandpaper: When you've got several layers of paint, lightly sand some of the top layer to expose the underlying color.*

~R

In this example, I'm using a clayboard to which I applied an acrylic texture with modeling paste (see Chapter 7) and then covered with a copper metallic surfacer (see Chapter 8).

1 Mix up some paint that's a little darker than your painted surface. I also like to mix in a bit of matte medium or gel to thin out the color and make it a little easier to work with.

2 Apply the darker paint with a paint brush, rag, or paper towel. Rub over the surface.

If you're painting over modeling paste or other texture, rub the darker color into the creases and edges.

3 Wait a few minutes for the paint to just start drying, then rub or roll off as much or as little of the paint to get the effect you want.

4 If the paint gets too dry, spritz it with a little water. If it's not completely dry, this will allow you to remove a little more paint.

5 *Rubbing* with a rag creates a cleaner, more subtle finish.

Rolling your rag or paper towel over the piece (instead of rubbing) gives you a more mottled surface.

—continued

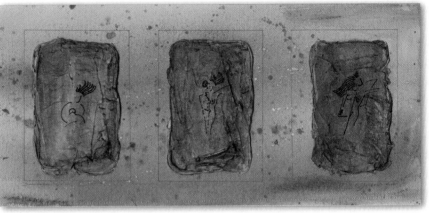

6 Make sure you don't take off *all* the paint or leave *too much* smeared around. You want a complex, rich look, but not a muddy one.

Take that rag or paper towel that you used to rub off the paint, and re-use it: rub its wet paint onto another substrate.

~ℛ

Example of rub and rag

For this piece, I painted watercolor paper with a wet-into-wet wash (a wet brush full of watercolor onto paper still wet with water or color). Then I spattered it with thick watercolor paint and a gold opaque marker to make an interesting background on which to apply the modeling paste. When the background was dry, I applied light modeling paste that I first tinted with a bit of acrylic paint.

Because I wanted definition in the ridges, I rubbed darker paint into the dry modeling paste to pop out its sculpted texture.

I wanted a kind of petroglyph look for this magazine spread, so when the paste was very dry, I drew stylized images directly on the textured panels with a Sharpie permanent pen.

My illustration was larger than my scanner glass, so I scanned the piece in two files. In Photoshop, I changed the opacity of the top layer to 50 percent so I could align the images perfectly. Then I set the opacity of the top layer back to 100 percent and flattened the image. *Voilà*, my illustration was perfectly mended.

I wanted this piece to have a feeling of antiquity, but with a contemporary edge that relates to today, thus the combination of rubbed texture and abstract, modern drawings.

This rough, sandy texture provides a tough background for this promo piece about clothing designed by Navy SEALs.

Also try this!

Glaze an entire textured surface by mixing a medium or gel into acrylic paint and brushing it everywhere (you can use hard gel mixed with acrylic paint to *create* and *paint* the texture in one step). When that's dry, take full-strength acrylic paint and liberally cover the more textural areas. This is usually very messy! Using soft paper towels or rags, carefully wipe off most of the surface paint, leaving thick paint only in the crevices. The texture immediately has more contrast and visual interest.

Or paint a surface with a liberal amount of wet paint (either transparent or opaque, depending on the effect you want) and then pull the paint off with wadded-up rags. Or roll wadded rags into the paint or even stamp into the wet paint with sponges, the rim of a drinking glass, cardboard edges—all kinds of things will pick up paint and create new shapes.

And don't throw away your paper towels! If you've got wet acrylic or watercolor on the towels, spread them out and spritz some water on them, or pour on a little water if you don't have a spritzer. The colors will all meld together and you'll have a lovely, textured paper to do something else with. ~R

Don't forget that when you pick up the paint with a paper towel or sponge or drinking glass or cardboard edge, you can use that item to stamp that paint onto yet another surface! ~R

The background for this illustration of Lady Macduff is a paper towel soaked with watery acrylic paint. I glued it to the back of the shadowbox with gel. I covered the front with another layer of lightly tinted soft gel, then used the pointy end of my brush to scrape more texture into it.

The ground she's walking on is tissue paper mushed with gel and acrylic paint. ~R

Rub paint into masking tape texture

Masking tape makes a quick, easy, and inexpensive layering medium that takes really well to the rubbing and ragging technique. ~R

1   On any kind of substrate, even a lamp shade or bond paper from your printer, layer pieces of masking tape. Tear them into differently sized strips, lay them all in one direction or crosswise or cattywampus—it's up to you.

2   Paint a first coat of acrylic paint over the masking tape. Rub off some of the paint here and there if you like.

3   Paint a second coat over the entire page or just a piece of it, and perhaps a third layer of paint. Experiment with different colors in different parts of the piece, depending on how you plan to use it in the final project. Rub and rag each coat.

The text for the headline of this small flyer is made of polymer clay. I used the letterform mold shown on page 192. ~R

11 Stamp Textures with Alcohol Inks

Tools and materials

- Glossy-coated paper or surface, preferably white and shiny
- Alcohol-based inks
- Krylon Leafing pens: silver, copper, or gold
- Either an alcohol ink applicator such as made by Adirondack (shown on the opposite page)

  OR make your own (explained in Steps 1–2) with a stamp block (small wooden block, as shown), sticky-back Velcro, and craft felt

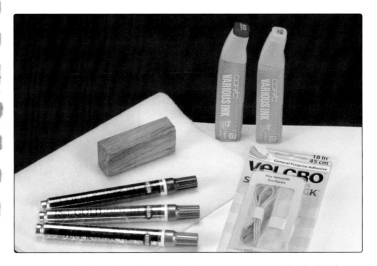

You can make lovely, rich, mottled textures using alcohol inks. Alcohol inks are designed to print onto slick surfaces, which means they are a great option for printing onto metal, glass, glossy paper, photographs, refrigerators, bald heads, or any other polished surface you can think of.

By stamping or dripping with these materials you can create stunning patterns and textures.

Before putting alcohol inks on an important object, such as a glossy photograph, always check on a hidden area to see how the alcohol ink reacts with that particular piece.

To make your own stamping tool, *you'll need some sticky-back Velcro and some type of stamping block.*

1   Cut a piece of the loopy Velcro to fit your stamping block. Stick it down nice and tight.

2   Cut a strip of inexpensive craft felt the very same size as your block. Affix it to the Velcro side of your stamping block.

Or you can buy a stamper *and replacement felts at a craft store.*

—continued

My friend, Billy McCubbin, had a bunch of extra scrap wood at his job and I happily turned them into perfect stamping blocks. However, if you don't have a pal with a pile of wood blocks to donate, use a Magic Rub eraser. It's the perfect size, is readily available, and costs next to nothing! ~C

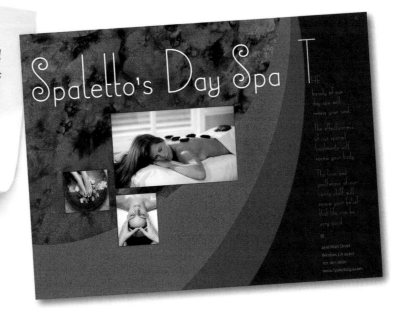

Create a pattern with alcohol inks

Alcohol inks are designed for slick surfaces, so use your imagination. You can use alcohol inks on any stamps you have as well.

1   Dab your craft felt pad with spots of alcohol inks in two or three colors.

2   If you have a metal leafing pen, dab the same surface with one of the pens.

3   Start lightly dabbing your ink-soaked pad on the coated paper. Overlap your stamped shapes and allow the ink to mingle on the coated paper.

Re-ink your pad as necessary and keep building your texture until you have developed the look you want. I like to mix the silver with the gold leafing inks for more interesting textures.

As you can see, these marbled textures are complex and rich!

TIP! *Because you are using a coated paper, it will take your texture a while to dry. If you have quite a juicy surface, a hair dryer might cause the ink to move and ruin your look (or improve it), so have patience.*

Try this!

More techniques to use with alcohol inks.

- Simply **drip the inks** from the bottle and let them mix on the slick surface to create interesting sort of "lava lamp" textures, as shown to the right.

- Drip or stamp or print an image with alcohol ink onto the **slick side of freezer paper,** then use that freezer paper as a stamp to offset the image onto another surface or two.

- Drip or stamp or print an image with alcohol ink on the back side of **a piece of plexiglass,** as shown below, then use another technique on the front of the acrylic for a great look of depth.

I took advantage of these alcohol ink drops to anchor the type, simulate the sun, and give a feeling of the summer heat. I bought three photos from iStockphoto.com, changed them to silhouettes in Photoshop, and put the ad together in Illustrator. I used a couple of symbols from the Illustrator Symbols Libraries to finish it off.

Above, I put the ink texture inside the text: In InDesign, I set the type, selected the text box with the black pointer tool, and chose "Create Outlines" from the Type menu. I placed the scan of the alcohol ink texture on the InDesign page and positioned it on top of the text. I then "cut" that texture, selected the outlined text, and used the "Paste Into" command from the Edit menu to put the texture inside the letterforms. ~R

12 Texturize with Absorbent Ground and Washi Paper

Tools and materials

- Watercolor palette
- Water
- Watercolors or acrylic paints
- Watercolor brushes
- Illustration board or other heavy substrate
- Matte medium
- Absorbent ground
- Modeling paste or gels
- Gesso
- A variety of thin washi (Japanese handmade paper) with lacy patterns, inclusions, and interesting textures

As much as I love my Arches 300 lb. watercolor paper, I also love to try out new products and experiment with other techniques, such as this one using a product called *absorbent ground*.

Absorbent ground is a medium in a jar that you can paint onto almost any substrate, which then makes that particular material accept water media. The results aren't anything close to what you get with uncoated watercolor paper, but for collaging and texture techniques, it's great.

Washi is very thin and delicate-looking Japanese tissue paper made from the bark of the gampi tree; although it looks and feels delicate, it's much tougher and more durable than paper made with wood pulp. Clothes and household products and toys are made with washi. In this project, we're going to combine absorbent ground and washi to create beautiful textures.

Play with the materials

After I have spread the absorbent ground on the substrate (as shown on the following page), I like to affix washi papers to emphasize wrinkles and torn edges. I glue these materials down with matte medium.

I keep a very casual, abstract, random surface and make sure not to cover the whole area. Then I drip and splatter with gesso and other acrylic media to get a totally varied and textural surface. Before my mediums are dry I may even sprinkle clean, dry, beach sand into areas.

Play with watercolor paper

My good friend, watercolor paper, comes out to play with a technique that allows us to actually get back to the white of the paper—almost. If watercolor paper is the substrate you plan to use with absorbent ground and washi, first coat its surface with matte medium and allow it to dry; this creates a barrier that prevents the pigment from settling into the fibers of the paper when you paint on it.

This means the watercolor paper no longer has the surface quality you expect when using regular transparent watercolor, but it does have great potential for some absolutely stunning, textural effects.

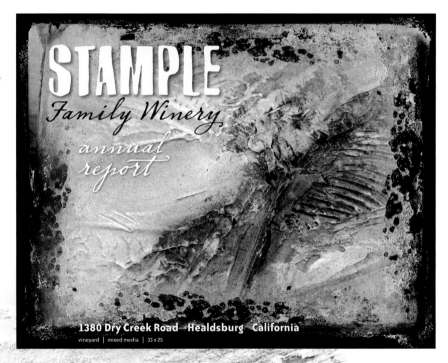

STAMPLE *Family Winery* *annual report*

1380 Dry Creek Road · Healdsburg · California
vineyard | mixed media | 33 x 25

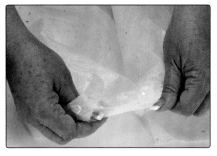

1 Choose some lovely washi papers—lacy, with bark, with threads, experiment with different kinds. Tear the washi paper into a variety of sizes and shapes.

2 Put a blob of absorbent ground on the substrate. I use a spackle knife, spreader, or even a little piece of mat board to smear everything around. It's better to be kind of loose and abstract with the ground. You want ridges and places for the paint to settle—don't be smooth and tidy.

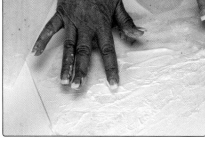

3 Glue washi papers to your substrate using the absorbent ground and/or matte medium as glue. Make big, rough-edged, overlapping shapes. Glue down thoroughly, but let wrinkles and texture show.

4 Don't be afraid to use your fingers to get everything affixed to the substrate.

Also try dressmaking tissue patterns in place of washi. They are thin and have interesting markings. ~*R*

Tip! *If you don't have washi paper handy, use white tissue paper, like the kind you use in gift wrapping. Colored tissue papers tend to bleed their colors, so keep that in mind— and take advantage of it!*

If you plan to completely paint over the texture so the washi won't show at all, definitely use the cheap tissue paper. ~*R*

5 I sometimes paint with the absorbent ground to get brush stroke textures. You might need to thin it with a little water.

6 Comb, stamp, scratch, poke into your textures to make more interesting places for paint to creep.

7 Once you're satisfied with your texture, let it air dry thoroughly. You can get out your trusty hair dryer and speed up the process, but because the absorbent ground is thick and the washi paper almost textile-like, using a hair dryer can take a while. You might want to just set this project aside and work on something else for awhile.

8 After your piece is bone dry, mix up some watercolor paint or thinned acrylics and start painting your texture. Because absorbent ground puts a coating on the substrate, it is much easier to work and rework paint until it is just what you want without worrying about destroying the surface underneath.

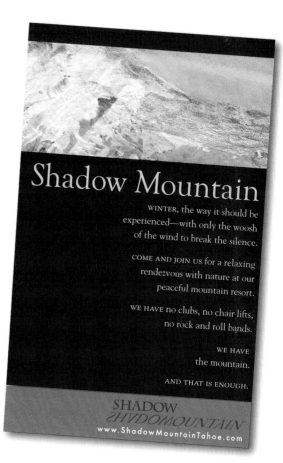

Try matte medium, washi, sand, and gesso

This is similar to the previous technique, but uses different art materials. Instead of matte medium, feel free to use polymer medium (it's glossy) or any of the gels. If you don't have clean beach sand handy, try the colored sands that you can find in craft stores.

1 Start as you did with the previous example, Step 1, but this time use matte medium instead of absorbent ground to crumple up and adhere the washi to the board.

2 Sprinkle sand on the piece while the matte medium is wet.

3 Spatter liberally with gesso, either clear or opaque white, depending on your desired result.

4 Let your piece dry thoroughly.

5 Mix up a bit of juicy, thick watercolor (transparent) or acrylic paint (opaque unless thinned with water or gel) and start painting your texture.

6 Layer your colors until the wrinkles and sand texture grab just enough pigment to show some contrast.

John Tollett opened this scan of the texture in Photoshop and ran the Poster Edges filter on it to pop out the textures even more dramatically before he created the handbill.

13 Make Textures with Monoprints

Tools and materials

- Piece of ¼" glass about 12" x 12" at the least (tape the edges to prevent injury)
- Palette or another piece of glass on which to roll ink
- Hard printmaking brayer at least 4" in width
- Printmaking inks (I prefer water-based inks for easy clean-up, although oil-based inks are wonderful and don't dry out while you work)
- Tub for soaking paper
- Sink and water
- Two old tea towels
- Printmaking paper (I prefer BFK) torn to the size of the glass
- Scratching and scraping tools such as a skewer, hotel card, embossing stylus, palette knife, etc.
- Stiff paint brush
- Squeegee
- Baren (or a clean brayer)

With monoprints you can create amazing, abstract textures that show brush strokes and subtle gradations at the same time.

The name "monoprint" means that you'll only get one print, a unique piece of art, out of each piece of painted glass. You'll usually be digitizing the resultant print, of course, but you could also use this technique to create similar but different *original* pieces to add to a small run of a digitally printed job.

For instance, let's say your corporate headquarters is having its annual luncheon for big buyers at a tony restaurant. You design lovely invitations along the lines of an art gallery opening. While 300 invitations are on the press, you create 15 monoprints, chop them into 20 pieces each, and tip one onto each invitation (attach it with a spot of glue) as if it's an original piece of art. Which it is.

The monoprint process

The supplies for monoprinting are very basic—a piece of glass, a palette, a hard brayer, several printing inks, and sheets of printmaking paper.

In this process, you'll roll ink onto your palette (I prefer to use another piece of glass as my palette) and apply that ink to a piece of glass. By rolling out inks with a "rainbow roll-up" (two or more inks rolled side by side that blend into a transition color), you can create lovely and subtle gradations.

As a contrast to that smoothness, I like to paint onto the glass with a stiff brush to get rough brush strokes.

When your ink is on the glass and designed to your satisfaction, you'll place a damp sheet of printmaking paper over the image and rub the paper. Then you'll peel away the paper from the glass to find the inky image transferred to the paper.

1 After tearing the printmaking paper into the size you want, place it in a tub of clean water and let it soak for a few minutes while you get your painted glass ready. (You'll use the paper in Step 6.)

2 Paint some color on your glass plate with the water-based printmaking inks. I also drip on some matte medium to keep things from drying out too quickly. In the example above, I'm adding some dashes of red acrylic paint.

3 Use your hard brayer to blend the colors together.

4 I use paint brushes to add textures and marks where I want them.

—*continued*

Tip! *If you are writing words in your paint, be sure to write them* **backwards** *because your final image will be reversed.*

5 Try using scraping tools, a spackle knife possibly, to create texture. How about using a comb? Try skewers or the edge of corrugated cardboard or steel wool or . . .

6 Take a sheet of paper out of the tub and pat it dry between two towels.

7 Lay the paper carefully over the image on the glass.

Tip! *One of the things I like to do with this technique is scratch or stamp into the paint after I roll it or paint it on the glass. I use my palette knife and all kinds of things to stamp into the paint—sponges, netting, lace, edges of old credit cards, Brillo pads, corrugated papers, bottoms of paper cups, etc. Look around your house or studio and see what you can find—you might be surprised at what can make an interesting pattern.*

8 Rub carefully all over the back of the paper with a brayer or baren.

If you put the paint on fairly thin and a little tacky, your image will transfer better. You need to press fairly hard to get the texture to show through. However, use a straight down and straight up motion—no smears.

9 Sometimes you can make a second print from the image if you have enough paint left. The second print will be even more abstract.

Or spritz water on the plate and lay a paper towel on it. Brayer and spritz the towel until it's colored (see Chapter 27).

Clean off the piece of glass with a paper towel and start over with another image.

Monoprints are always a surprise to me.
I often only use a piece of the print in my graphics.

14 Make Textures with Bubbles

Tools and materials
- Sheets of printmaking paper
- A small container the size of your sheets of paper
- Dishwashing liquid
- Drinking straw
- Marbling paints

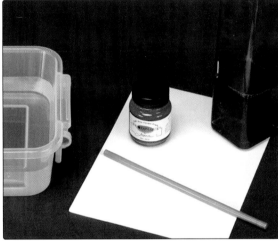

This is a fun texture to make; however, it's a bit trickier than it looks. First you need to get the right proportions of dishwashing liquid to water (four to one). Then you need to make sure you use the right pigments (marbling paints). You need a paper that works with water and has a smooth texture (such as printmaking paper).

I've already made all the mistakes for you, so you should come out with perfectly amazing bubble textures if you follow my hard-earned tips.

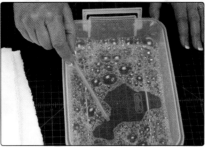

1   Tear your printmaking paper into sheets that will fit your container.

2   Make a mixture of dishwashing liquid and water: four parts water to one part dishwashing liquid.

3   Your mixture should be kind of creamy. You want rather tough bubbles and if your proportions aren't quite right, your bubbles will break too quickly.

4   Pour in your marbling paint. Make sure you create a rich color because the results tend to be delicate and you want to see something on your page.

5   Use your drinking straw to make a substantial sheet of bubbles. Blow slowly—you want nice large bubbles and not just a bunch of froth.

6   Hold your paper perfectly flat and lower it quickly onto the layer of bubbles. Do not let your paper hit the surface of the liquid—bubbles only.

7   Your paper will show the delicate bubble print.

Of course, you can repeat the process with bubbles of another color and make richer, more complex patterns.

Also consider using this technique in combination with other background textures.

Combine Techniques!

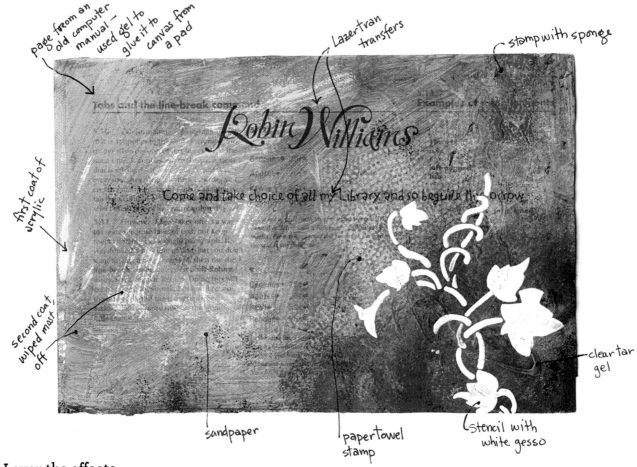

page from an old computer manual — used gel to glue it to canvas from a pad

Lazertran transfers

stamp with sponge

first coat of acrylic

Second coat, wiped most off

sandpaper

paper towel stamp

clear tar gel

stencil with white gesso

Layer the effects

The most fun of all is layering a whole bunch of effects to get the look you need for your project.

If you get to a point where you hate it or a piece of it is looking muddy, just take some white gesso, paint it on or use a putty knife to texture it on, and start over—either on the entire piece or just the part you don't like.

This is not a finished project (above), but a sampling of various techniques used together to encourage you to get out all the paints and tools and have at it.

Some of the techniques used above are explained in other chapters; check the index.

PART 3

Paint Textures

With an open mind and gleeful experimentation, you will find there are so many marvelous techniques you can try with transparent watercolors or opaque acrylics that can become part of your design repertoire. You, the designer, need to choose what is exciting, comfortable, and effective for your particular way of working.

There are many ways to do things in this world, and that includes creating paint textures for graphic design.

FIREFLY
Bar & Grill

Paint Textures

Although we show you each technique individually, keep in mind they are most exciting when used together and overlaid.

15 Salt the Paint

Simple table salt adds a great dynamic to watercolor.

See pages 76-77.

16 Blow the Paint

Use a straw to blow the paint into spidery tendrils.

See pages 78-79.

17 Spray the Paint

Use a water spritzer to spray water into wet paint and bleed it.

See pages 80-81.

18 Pour the Paint

Pour paint onto paper to get beautiful graduated tones.

See pages 82-85.

19 Scratch the Paint

Scratch into paint to create definition in otherwise random shapes.

See pages 86-89.

20 Sponge the Paint

Sponge into the wet paint to create a range of organic texture.

See pages 90-93.

21 Splatter the Paint

Throw some paint onto that paper!

See pages 94-97.

Ever since I was a young student, I have loved the beauty and challenge of water media. I love the unpredictability and luminosity one can achieve with this media and have pursued learning about and painting in watercolors to this day. My dear friend Tosya Shore and I get together every Friday afternoon we possibly can and paint together. Every year we attend workshops to experiment with new information and techniques. We paint abstract texture-based pieces, illustrations, and traditional landscape paintings. It's a fascinating ride—and we get to discuss our lives as we paint away. ~C

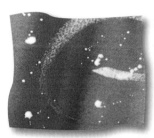

22 Paint with Resist

Sketch elements onto the paper that *won't* get painted.

See pages 98–101.

23 Stamp-Resist into the Paint

Stamp random texture into the paint.

See pages 102–105.

24 Bleach the Paint

Use bleach to create intriguing designs in the paint.

See pages 106–109.

25 Tape and Paint

Use good ol' masking tape to create painted texture.

See pages 110–111.

26 Plastic Wrap and Paint

Let plastic wrap or plastic bags create the texture.

See pages 112–113.

27 Paper Towels and Paint

Don't neglect your trusty paper towels as design elements.

See pages 114–115.

15 Salt the Paint

Tools and materials

- Watercolors
- Watercolor paper
- Watercolor palette
- Water
- Brushes (not shown)
- Hair dryer (not shown)
- Table salt, kosher salt, sea salt, or any kind of salt

This is an old, tried-and-true technique that can be hokey at worst and quite delightful at best. The science behind this technique is that salt sucks water to itself, and because salt is a crystal, it not only sucks up the water, but leaves a crystalline image behind. If you sprinkle table salt into damp, darkish wash (a wet layer of paint), within seconds you'll see little snowflake images appear.

This seems foolproof, but of course, it isn't. For this technique to work, make sure you don't *pour* the salt on, and when you *sprinkle* the salt, you have to do it at exactly the right moment. You want to put the salt on when the wash has just lost the sheen of the water and not a second before. But don't wait until the wash is too dry—nothing will happen if your wash is too dry.

1 Create a good, heavy wash on a sheet of watercolor paper. For the effect to be visible, use mid-tones to dark colors.

2 The key to getting this effect to work is the wetness of the wash. If it's too wet, you'll have minimal results; if the wash is too dry, you'll have minimal to no results.

The wash has to be just right: When the wet sheen has just gone off the paint, but the paint is still damp, sprinkle grains of salt onto it.

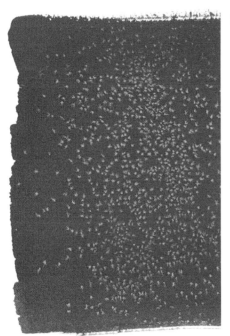

3 Allow the wash to dry with the salt in place. It is important to let everything dry completely because the grains of salt can hold on to pigment and smear if they are even slightly damp.

4 When completely dry, carefully brush the salt off your piece.

Tip!

Different types of salt give different results. Experiment!

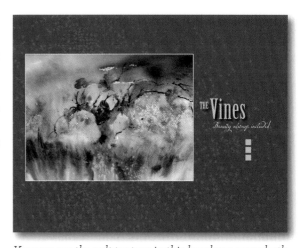

You can see the salt texture in this brochure cover both in the inset watercolor painting and on the background. The background is the red piece you see in the example. In InDesign, I placed it on top of a solid black rectangle, gave the red salted piece an opacity of 44 percent, and changed its effect to luminosity (from the Effects panel). It's great to have both the handmade elements and the digital tools!

16 Blow the Paint

Tools and materials

- Watercolors or acrylics that you've watered down
- Watercolor paper or other paintable substrate
- Watercolor palette
- Water
- Brushes
- Drinking straw or other thin paper tube

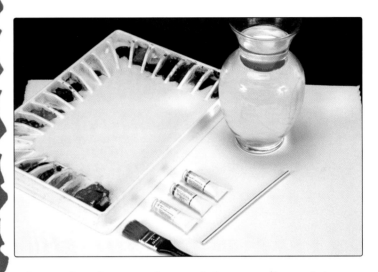

When my friend Tosya and I attended a watercolor workshop by Lian Quan Zhen, we were fascinated to watch this artist blow the paint around and even use his fingers as he created his fresh, spontaneous paintings. His control was absolutely amazing!

I have better control of where my paint ends up by blowing through a drinking straw, but experiment and see what you can do—use your fingers, a hair dryer, let the rain fall on the wet paint, tilt the paper, add texture to the substrate and let the paint work its way through it. The spidery tendrils have lots of possibilities as graphic elements.

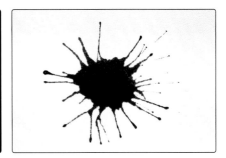

1   Start with a dry sheet of watercolor paper. Sometimes I use an already painted surface, but it must be dry.

2   Drop a large puddle of watercolor paint onto the sheet of paper.

3   Take a drinking straw and blow the paint out to the sides of the puddle. With a little practice, you can become quite skilled at controlling the shape and length of the spindly tendrils.

4   Or fill up your cheeks with air and give the puddle of paint a good hard blow. Repeat until you have the paint where you want it.

On this piece of masonite I layered acrylic paint (some of which I rubbed off), pumice gel, regular gel; I sponged, scraped, and blew the paint around in several places, creating an organic look. The moth wings are from a dead moth on the windowsill. ~R

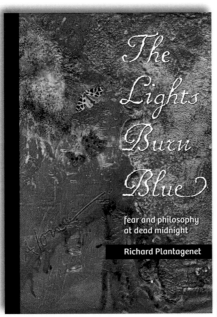

Because I'm a digital designer, I didn't have to risk ruining my lovely watercolor by blowing a splat of paint on it. In InDesign, I placed the splat scan (a TIFF) over the water-color image and applied the Multiply effect (from the Effects palette) to make the white paper transparent. ~C

17 Spray the Paint

Tools and materials

- Watercolors
  or acrylic paints
- Watercolor palette
- Watercolor paper
- Brushes
- Water in spray bottle

This technique involves a willingness to make a mess; you at least want to protect your table from running paint. And there's no way to predict the outcome, so you need to be willing to take a risk on what shows up on the page!

When you're creating textures for graphic design pieces, don't worry about creating a finished, lovely painting to hang on your wall. Most of my finished textures look like unfinished sloppy messes, but I can always find a particularly interesting edge or lucky color accident that is just right. I scan just that little part and use it for a piece. You don't have to *master* these techniques in a pictorial kind of way to use them as provocative effects in your design work.

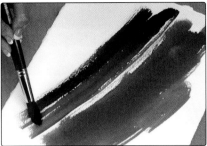

1 Put a fairly heavy swath of paint on your substrate. You don't want it too sloppy-wet, but neither do you want dry-brush (paint on a dry brush on dry paper). Leave white paper at the edge.

2 Add another color if you like, so you have more options with color possibilities. Don't let it dry.

3 Take your spray bottle and just spray along the edge of the wet paint. You will see a fringe develop with little rivulets running into the white paper.

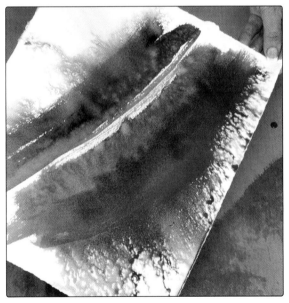

4 Tip your paper to encourage the paint to run and drip off that fringe.

Where the terroso meets the sea

Pasquale Island

₁₈ Pour the Paint

Tools and materials

- Watercolors in red, yellow, and blue
- Watercolor paper
- Little bowls
- Water
- Brushes
- Tray

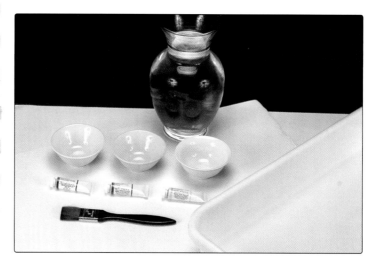

This technique is a bit on the messy side, but it's so satisfying to see the colors flow together and mix on the page. To make a background that really looks good, however, you need to be quick and know when to stop. It is very easy to play a little too long and end up with a muddy mess rather than shimmery colors with beautifully feathered edges.

An approach that works well is to start with primary colors and then proceed to more sophisticated mixtures down the road once you get the hang of how the paints mix.

One technique that combines nicely with pouring paint is to first splatter and paint over the white paper (see Chapter 21), and *then* pour paint over your design.

A nice heavy watercolor paper is good for this technique because it is a little easier to control the flow of the paint if your paper is a bit stiff.

Mix your watercolor paint in small bowls with a little water. **To create vivid, brilliant color,** make sure your paint is slightly on the creamy side (as opposed to watery).

Mix up at least ⅓ cup of each color for a quarter sheet of watercolor paper. Watercolors dry much lighter than they look when wet, so if your paint is too watery, you'll end up with very pale backgrounds.

1   While you mix up your colors, soak your watercolor paper for several minutes in clean water.

2   Dry your paper with a clean towel, and empty the tray of water.

—continued

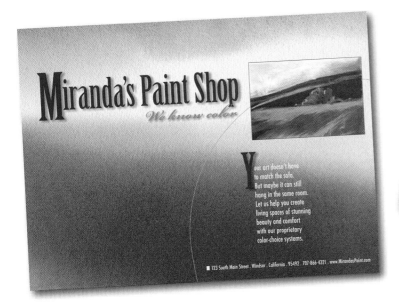

Don't wait until the moment you need a colorful background— grab another designer and make a day of slinging paint around so you have a pile of pages of all sorts ready to go when you need them. ~R

3 Holding the paper over the empty tray, pour your first paint color onto part of the damp sheet of watercolor paper and tip the color around. Don't cover the entire page.

Try to save the leftover color and pour it back into your little bowl.

4 Pour a bit of your next color onto a white area of the page and again tip your paper around to let the color flow and mix a bit with your other color.

Leave some of the paper white for the third color.

5 Pour on your third color and keep tipping and directing the flow until you get what you want. Be careful that you don't mix everything together—not attractive, believe me.

You can spray a little water to help the flow and get rid of little white spots. But don't fiddle and touch the paint too much as it will get kind of mottled and not have that pretty, flowy look.

Tip! *If you have paint left in your little cups, fold up a few paper towels and dip them in the colors to dye them. Or mop up the surplus paint with paper towels, then hang the towels to dry and use in another project. See Chapter 27.* ~R

Also try this!

Watercolor pretty much terrifies me—Carmen and I have interesting stories about our adventures in this medium. Carmen's actually an artist and is brilliant with watercolor, but I much prefer acrylic paint because it's not so fussy or demanding. ~*R*

- Pour acrylic paint (fluid acrylics work particularly well; see page 17) onto a plexiglass or glass surface. When dry (above, right), you can peel it up with a putty knife and use it on a collage.

- Pour fluid acrylics (or watered-down regular acrylics) onto a surface already textured; tilt the piece as the paint scurries through the surface structure. Try texturing with a gel that has stuff in it, such as little glass beads or pumice.

- Pour small amounts of various fluid acrylics in a paper cup. Do not stir the colors together, then pour from the cup onto a substrate (as shown to the right).

- Paint a plexiglass or glass surface with several layers of a gloss gel or polymer medium (the glossier it is, the more transparent it will be). Let it dry between each layer. Then drip the acrylic paint on the gel or medium. When dry, you will be able to peel it up and apply it somewhere else as a transparent decal; glue it on with more gel or medium.

• poetry slam • marc smith • hear with your eyes • living art •
sunday • noon to midnight • nuyorican poets cafe • alphabet city

every sunday in october

In Photoshop, I altered the colors of this poured paint with the Hue/Saturation panel and took just this corner to use in the postcard above.

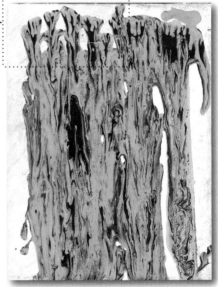

19 Scratch the Paint

Tools and materials

- Watercolors or acrylics
- Watercolor paper
- Watercolor palette
- Water
- Brushes
- Matte medium
- Scraping and scratching tools such as X-acto knife, pocket knife, razor blade, credit card, stylus

Watercolor can be such an abstract medium with its generally soft edges and transparent colors. By scratching into the wet paint, you can create definition in otherwise soft areas.

When my first watercolor teacher, Mr. Nye, took his trusty old pocket knife out of his pocket and proceeded to scrape beautiful tree branches into his nice dark wash, I was sold on scratching. Of course when Mr. Nye did it, it looked so easy. I soon discovered that elegant scratching isn't quite as simple as it looks. You have to be patient, vigilant, and a little gutsy to create good-looking scratches!
~C

Scratch the paint

The first thing you must do is choose the right tool for the scratch you want. If you are scratching a light mark into a dark damp wash, you need a kind of dull scratching tool like the end of a paintbrush or a dull pocketknife blade. You are basically pushing the paint out of the line—kind of like a squeegee.

If you want a crisp, clean scratch into a dry area of paint, use an X-acto knife, razor blade, or sharp pocket knife.

Also pay attention to the wetness or dryness of your paper: If your wash is too wet when you try to scratch into it, the paint will seep back into your mark and you will be left with a dark mark in your wash. This can be a great effect in itself, but if you're looking for a nice light mark in your dark wash, this will be disappointing.

If your wash isn't damp enough, you won't get anything at all.

So experiment, but pay attention to your results! *(Robin, who has a terrible relationship with fussy watercolors, says, "Try acrylics!")*

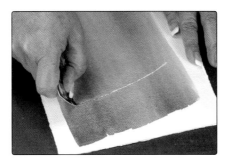

- Create a dark wash on your watercolor substrate and allow it to dry just enough so the sheen is off the paper.

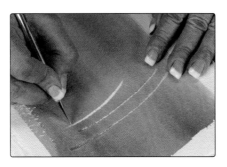

Effect two

For this effect, you will essentially squeegee the paint out of the area, so use a slightly dull tool. Create a dark wash, but when the paint is still quite damp, scratch into the paint with your pointy object to create a lighter mark.

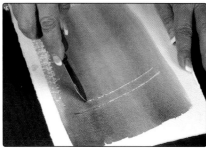

Effect one

Take a sharp tool, such as an X-acto knife or pocket knife, and scratch into the dry paint, back to the paper. Your paper surface is now damaged, so do this technique as the last step on the piece.

GRiFFER
A PLACE FOR PETS

OPEN HOUSE! • SATURDAY & SUNDAY • MARCH 17–18
10 A.M. TO 5 P.M. • 241 ST. FRANCIS DRIVE

Other paint scratching techniques

Try acrylics! says Robin

Acrylics paints, as opposed to watercolors, provide a lot more body and
a lot more time in which to scrape,
especially if you mix the paint with
a gel or medium (see page 17) to
make it thicker and take longer to dry.

1 If you want a background, first lay
   down a coat of acrylic paint using
   any of the techniques in this book.
   Let it dry.

2 Paint over the first coat with
   acrylic mixed with gel. You don't
   need to paint the entire piece.

3 Use the end of the brush or any
   other tool to scrape patterns or
   words into the paint.

- **Rub paint into the scratches:**
  If you like, after the scratched
  paint is thoroughly dried, layer
  more paint of a contrasting color;
  then before the new paint dries,
  use a damp paper towel to wipe
  away most of the wet paint, letting
  it stay in the scratched areas (see
  Chapter 10).

Roswell Association of Grief Counselors *annual report*

Freezer-paper scratch prints

Use freezer paper and your scratched-in acrylic image as a stamp to print onto something else for another effect.

1   Add gel or acrylic glazing liquid to your acrylic paint to make it stay moist longer. Paint with the acrylic onto wax paper or the shiny side of a piece of freezer paper, the kind you buy at the grocery store or get from the butcher.

2   While the acrylic paint is wet and gooey, use any pointy object to draw patterns into the paint, write words *backwards,* draw little pictures, scratch textures, etc.

3   While the image is still wet, turn the paper over and use it as you would a rubber stamp onto another painted substrate—rub it gently onto the substrate. Depending on how wet it is, you can probably stamp a pattern onto two or three substrates, including any of your watercolor pieces or onto a paper towel. Each print becomes more abstract.

The point is that you can scrape and scratch into any wet surface to develop more texture, to write words, to create a subliminal message, etc. Combine this with several of the other techniques in this book—the combinations are endless! ~R

20 Sponge the Paint

Tools and materials

- Watercolors or acrylics
- Watercolor paper
- Watercolor palette
- Water
- Brushes
- Natural sponges or old kitchen sponge

You can't beat beautiful natural sponges for making some great textural effects. You can buy these amazing tools in sets at your local art supply store or you can get some really fine, large varieties at your beauty and bath shops and even at health food stores.

If you don't have fancy natural sponges on hand, use an old sponge from your kitchen!

~R

Sponging is simple, but to really get effects that are worth the effort, you must pay attention to how wet your paper is and how liquid your paint is. This might take a little practice.

If everything is too wet, you'll end up with some gentle tonal blends and no texture. If everything is too dry, your colors might not bleed together and you'll end up with a very busy, kind of prickly texture.

As graphic designers, we set type on our pages, and busy textures can be difficult to work with. Spend a little time to experiment and get the technique down; it's worth it in the long run.

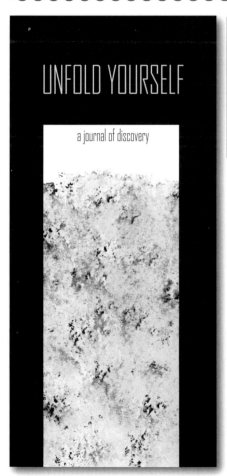

Once you've created several pages of sponged color, you'll find myriad ways to use them in your design work.

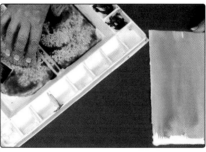

1 Start with a dry sheet of watercolor paper or a dry color wash in a light to mid value.

2 Mix up a palette of darker, slightly thick paint.

I like to mix my own colors; above, I am making a purplish-blue color by mixing in a bit of Alizarin Crimson with my Ultramarine Blue. I don't mix them thoroughly—I want all kinds of tones and shades on the tips of my sponge.

—continued

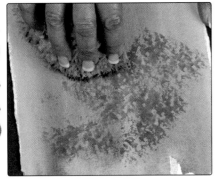  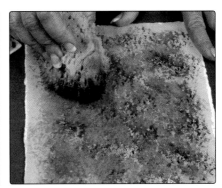

3 Lightly dip a natural sponge into the thick paint and "stamp" gently on the paper.

Sometimes I make single, distinct stamps, but other times I move around the whole wash and overlap marks to make a texture.

4 Let your first layer dry. Then repeat the process with layers of different values or colors to make a beautiful multidimensional effect.

Tip: *Sometimes you'll want a softer, more subtle effect. In that case, start with a slightly damp sheet of watercolor paper or a slightly damp watercolor wash. Make your paint a little thinner and lighter in value. This variation allows the colors to bleed together slightly and gives a more blended texture.*

Also see Chapter 18 on pouring watercolor where you can get a lovely graduated blend between the colors.

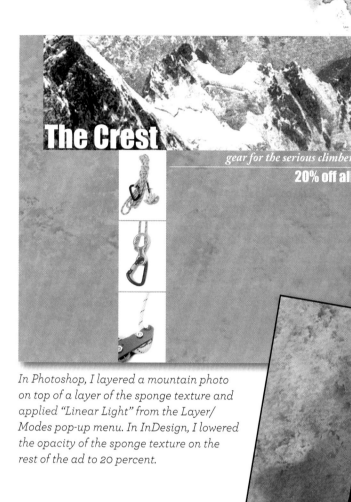

One of my favorite childhood memories
is standing in the market in Athens
with my mother and two little sisters,
buying sponges from a delightful old
Greek gentleman who looked like he
was in the movies—white hair,
large mustache, and of course
the de rigueur Greek
fishing hat.

~C

In Photoshop, I layered a mountain photo
on top of a layer of the sponge texture and
applied "Linear Light" from the Layer/
Modes pop-up menu. In InDesign, I lowered
the opacity of the sponge texture on the
rest of the ad to 20 percent.

For this hang tag,
in InDesign I overlaid a page of
sponge texture onto a soft watercolor wash so I could play with the
color interaction and placement,
giving me a great combination
of sky and water.

21 Splatter the Paint

Tools and materials

- Watercolors or acrylics
- Paint palette
- Watercolor paper
- Water
- Paint brushes
- Stencil brushes
- Toothbrushes
- Masking fluid
- Metallic pens

Splattering is a great effect. You can certainly use Photoshop or Illustrator to make splattered texture, but it doesn't look quite the same as the splatter you do with paint or ink. Nor is it nearly as much fun.

On paper, you can get many different effects depending on the tools you use, how wet or dry your substrate is, and how thick or watery your paint or ink is.

I love to splatter—it roughens things up and blends different colors and paint together. I take my paint and my faithful old dropcloth out onto the deck, away from the white walls and my neatnik husband. Often the most successful splatters are those made with large swinging motions of the arms, and if I'm worried about messing up the furniture, I tend to be timid and my splatters don't have the energy of a full arm swing.

Effect one

One of the easiest ways to get a splatter is to fill your brush with a lot of juicy paint and then hit your hand while your brush is positioned over your paper. I tend to use my favorite media, watercolors, but you can use acrylics just as easily.

Effect two

Put a wash (a wet brushful) of water or color on your watercolor paper and let it dry until the sheen is gone. Dip your old toothbrush, bristly stencil brush, or other tool into thick paint. Splatter it into the wash using your fingers, another brush, or by swinging your arm. If your wash is still damp enough, your splatters will get interesting "bleed" edges to them.

Effect three

I don't use a lot of opaque watercolors, but I do use white— I particularly like it for splattering. I keep a little bottle of Dr. Martin's Opaque White on hand because it's all mixed up and ready to go. Just use the dropper in the bottle to dribble it on the paper.

—continued

Stencil or stipple brushes.

I like to layer splatters—some on a damp wash, some on dry paper, some made with a brush splatter, some made with a toothbrush splatter, and sometimes my last layer with opaque marker pens.

~C

Effect four

Use masking fluid (which you can buy in a little jar at the art store) to splatter the white paper, let it dry, and then apply color. Wherever the masking fluid landed, those areas will remain the white of the paper.

Or first paint a wash on the paper and let it dry thoroughly. Then splatter the masking fluid, let it dry, and paint over the area with a darker wash. Let the new paint dry, then use your rubber cement pickup to remove the masking fluid (as explained in more detail in the next chapter).

Effect five

Some of the opaque pens and markers make terrific splattering tools—shake them well, then give a brisk snap to throw the ink on the paper. The metallic pens are great, but there are other colors available too. The white opaque pens are some of my favorites.

Of course, you could use opaque watercolors or acrylic paint, but the pens are easy and leave very nice, opaque splatters.

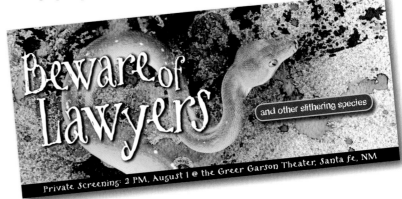

Beware of Lawyers

and other slithering species

Private Screening: 2 PM, August 1 @ the Greer Garson Theater, Santa Fe, NM

The piece of splattered paint gives the impression of a beach in this sunscreen promo piece.

I wanted a lot of energy in this background so I used a variety of techniques, including sponging, splattering, resist, and a bit of spraying.

97

22 Paint with Resist

Use an art masking fluid as a *resist* for watercolor: You'll paint on the resist fluid, let it dry, then paint over it. Wherever the resist is, the paint does not cover that area (it *resists* the paint).

There are many types of these liquid, rubbery materials. Sometimes you'll hear them referred to as "liquid frisket."

The colorless fluid dries clear, but some people prefer the kind with a tint so you can see where you've applied it.

My personal favorite masking fluid is made by Winsor & Newton. I've never had a problem with this brand, but I have seen some that rip the surface right off a painting—very distressing. Be sure to test your paper/resist combo before smearing an unfamiliar product all over your work.

Take care of your brushes

Art masking fluid wreaks havoc on paint brushes because it dries quickly and gets stuck in your ferrule (the metal piece that holds the bristles in place). I recommend that you dedicate certain brushes to art masking fluid—you don't want to ruin good brushes. Be sure to wash out even a dedicated brush immediately with soap and water after using this material. You can also use an **art masking pen,** such as MasquePen, instead of a brush and the liquid; check your local art or craft store. It works the same.

 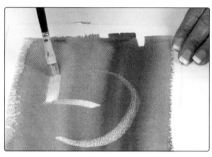 

1 Start with a dry sheet of watercolor paper. You can use masking fluid over an already painted surface, but always make sure the surface is totally dry before you slather it with the resist.

Tip! *If you don't have a **rubber cement pickup** (shown above), you can make one in a minute: Just pour some rubber cement or some of the resist fluid into a little blob and let it dry. Roll it up and there's your pickup.*

2 With the masking fluid, paint the area of color that you want to save.

Wait until the masking fluid is thoroughly dry, or use a hair dryer to speed things along.

3 Once everything is dry, paint over the masking fluid with your next wash of paint.

Resist the temptation to remove the masking fluid and see what your piece looks like until it's *completely* dry. If you grab that rubber cement pickup too early and start taking the mask off, little areas that aren't dry can smudge and ruin the effect.

4 You can layer your masking and painting until you achieve the desired result; for instance, you might want to splatter some resist on the page. It just requires patience to let things dry well (then again, don't wait more than 24 to 48 hours!).

5 Finally, when you feel you have completed the piece and everything is thoroughly dry, take a rubber cement pickup or soft eraser and gently rub off the dried resist. It comes off in rubbery crumbs (I won't mention what we call these in class).

Wax resist

Wax has been used by batik artists for years as a great resist.

I like to use wax on rough or cold press watercolor paper because it emphasizes the handmade line.

Unlike batik, with this process the wax is not melted; it is used cold.

Wax is easy to use, but one thing you must remember is that once you put the wax down, there is no going back—you can't get that wax off and make the paper accept more pigment.

Do not use a hair dryer to dry the wash because the melted wax will stain the surface of your paper.

1 Start with a dry sheet of water-color paper. You can use an already painted surface, but it must be dry.

Take an edge of a white candle, a piece of paraffin, a clear wax crayon from an egg-coloring kit, or any other wax you can find, and draw your desired shapes or designs onto your paper.

Press firmly, but not too hard—you don't really want to grind the wax into your piece.

2 Paint over your drawing with watercolor or acrylic washes. You will see the waxy images resist the paint.

You can see how a closeup of the wax resist texture (right) adds interest and richness to Lauren's CD cover. The cover above seems drab by comparison.

Shelf-liner resist

You might have some shelf liner in your cupboard, the kind with a self-adhesive back. This is great to use as a form of resist. If you have clear shelf liner, that's great—if not, use whatever you have. You're going to peel it off at the end of the process.

1   Use a substrate on which you've already painted a layer or applied another technique. Or create a new painted piece.

2   Cut out shapes from the shelf liner.

3   Lightly stick the shapes onto the painted substrate.

4   Paint over the page again using watercolor or acrylic (depending on what your substrate is) with the same color or a completely different one. It's okay if the paint gets underneath the edges—it creates a great textured edge. When dry, peel off the liner.

•   In fact, a similar technique is to make *sure* the paint gets underneath the liner. Mush the paint around under the shape, then with a paper towel or rag wipe off the paint *from the rest of the page.* What is underneath the liner will be darker instead of lighter.

You can use **masking tape** as a resist as well, as shown on pages 110–111.

Tip! *You can do this on any surface you can paint on—walls, doors, large coffee cups, etc. Don't limit yourself to merely paper. You're a digital designer, so think about incorporating any physical piece you can photograph or scan into your textural work.*

The substrate above is ready for another technique or to be scanned and used in a project.

I first painted this small piece a creamy color, then applied squarish shapes of shelf liner and painted it yellow. After I peeled off the liner pieces, I sponged them a bit with a sponge dipped in the yellow paint so they wouldn't be so stark. Then I painted the greenery onto a piece of freezer paper and stamped that onto the paper (see page 89). Now it looks like it's wanting some details inked in and collage figures applied to tell a story (see page 196).

23 Stamp-Resist into the Paint

Tools and materials

- Watercolors or acrylics
- Watercolor paper or other substrate
- Paint palette
- Brushes
- Water
- Matte medium
- Stamps: purchased; made by you by carving out a relief image on rubber, eraser, foam, cardboard; or materials you find in your environment

Stamping with a variety of materials and tools using watercolors or acrylics is lots of fun. And it can be the source of endless experimentation that results in colorful and interesting pages for you to work with in your digital design.

I usually make all my own stamps or use things I find laying around. Of course, you can purchase stamps at the crafts store, and sometimes iconographic images might be just what you are looking for, but I find that most of the pre-made stamps in the store are too darling for the serious designer. I have bought some batik stamps from Indonesia that I use, and now and then a geometric or logo-like image from the hobby store will work. But for the most part, I make the stamp myself out of things I find in the studio, the garage, the kitchen, the yard . . . .

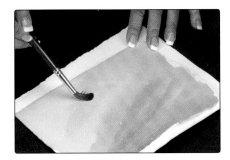

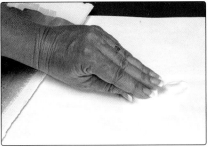

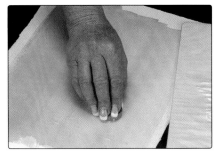

1 Create a medium to dark wash (layer of watery paint) on your watercolor paper. Allow it to dry only slightly.

2 Mix some matte medium and water on your palette or a plate.

> **To create a very distinct pattern,** add very little water to the medium or none at all.

> **To create an indistinct image,** mix up to an equal amount of matte medium and water.

Dip your stamping tool into the matte medium mixture (shown above). I'm using a little foam circle that came with my new box of CDs.

3 Stamp gently but firmly onto your not-quite-dry wash.

—continued

Tip! Things made out of foam make good stamps for this technique because they absorb just enough of the matte medium and watercolor paint to hold the color.

*The stamps at the crafts store designed for stamping your **walls** with acrylic paints are made from a fairly hard foam instead of rubber.*

Consider using anything as a stamp that will make a pattern or texture!

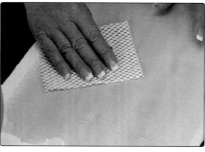

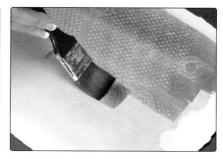

4 Try stamping with other things you find around the house. Here I'm using a spongy drawer liner that has a nice grid pattern.

5 Overlap your shapes for a nice random texture. Let everything dry thoroughly. You won't see much of your stamped images yet.

6 Paint over the piece with a darker wash. Now you will see your stamped images appear because the matte medium acts as a resist.

7 To give your piece added depth, add more stamps with darker paint: After your wash has dried, dab your stamping materials in thicker, darker paint and press onto the paper.

8 As we know in graphic design, repetition is your friend, so I'm stamping with my little circle stamp again. You can do this with or without the matte medium, depending on whether you plan to paint over it again.

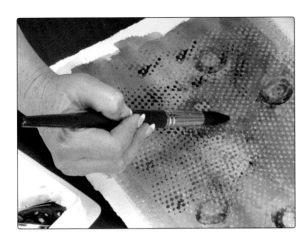

9 As a last step, I like to blend some of my shapes and edges with a little paint and water to unify the piece.

(Acrylics, when dry, become plastic and are impervious to water, so this step won't pick up any of the underlying paint.)

Among all the things you can use as stamps, don't forget about those thin sheets of soft foam you can buy in a craft store. Cut into the edges, roll it up, and stamp away. Or cut out pieces in shapes to use as stamps—glue them onto pieces of wood or the bottoms of coffee cups. These foam pieces are great to use in this resist technique.

24 Bleach the Paint

Tools and materials

- Watercolors
- Watercolor paper or other substrate
- Watercolor palette
- Water
- Pen you can fill with liquid
  Hair dryer (not shown)
- Household bleach

You can create beautiful, pale lines in your watercolor background with bleach. The lines usually have nice dark edges and will be smooth so you can paint over them with other transparent colors.

Use bleach very judiciously—it can eat holes in your paper just like it can eat holes in your clothes, so don't expect to keep using bleach over and over in the same area or you'll end up with a peekaboo effect that might not be what you are looking for.

Be careful—I've had some bad experiences with bleach! Make sure you aren't wearing your favorite jeans, working with your priceless Persian carpet underfoot, or drinking 7UP out of a glass similar to the one you've poured bleach into.

Also, don't use your good watercolor brushes—bleach will destroy them before your very eyes! You will be left in tears as all those expensive bristles fall out. Brushes with synthetic bristles seem to be oblivious to bleach.

1   Paint a heavy wash on a sheet of watercolor paper. This technique seems to work best when the color is on the darker side—even black is a good choice.

2   Allow the wash to dry thoroughly, or use your hair dryer to speed up the process.

3   Take a pen you can fill with liquid (art stores carry them) and carefully fill it with bleach.

4   Make marks into your dark wash. You'll see light marks appear; often they will have darker edges. Of course, it depends on the pigments in your initial wash as to what color emerges. Consequently, it's a good idea to experiment on a piece of scrap paper before applying bleach willy-nilly to your original.

You might be thinking, "Hey, how about those bleach pens you can buy at the supermarket?" I tried one of those. The problem is that in addition to the bleach in those pens, there is a little detergent as well. Unfortunately for an artist, that creates splotchy images that look a little diseased, plus it cracks. I do like all sorts of grungy effects, but this isn't one of them. ~C

But those bleach pens are great to use on photos! See page 109! ~R

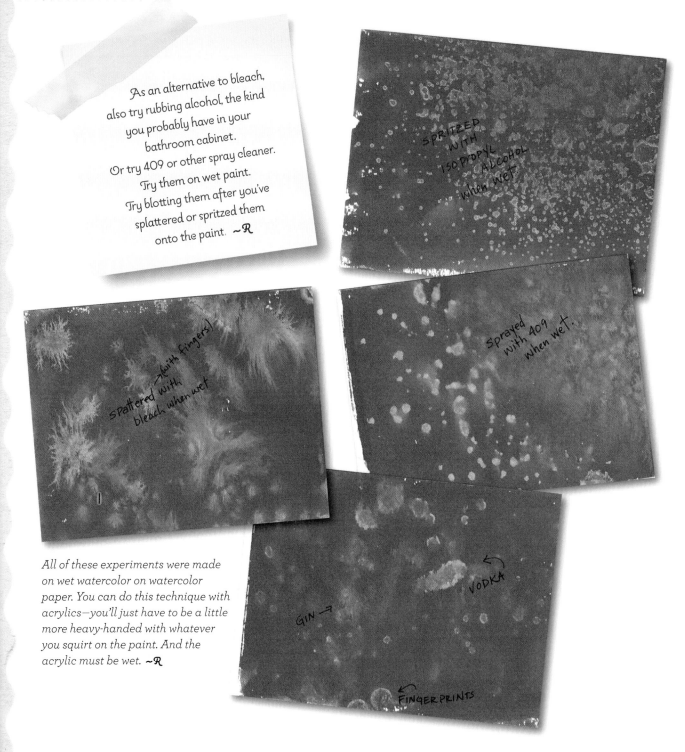

As an alternative to bleach,
also try rubbing alcohol, the kind
you probably have in your
bathroom cabinet.
Or try 409 or other spray cleaner.
Try them on wet paint.
Try blotting them after you've
splattered or spritzed them
onto the paint. ~R

SPRITZED
WITH
ISOPROPYL
ALCOHOL
when wet

Spattered with (with fingers)
bleach when wet

Sprayed
with 409
when wet.

All of these experiments were made
on wet watercolor on watercolor
paper. You can do this technique with
acrylics—you'll just have to be a little
more heavy-handed with whatever
you squirt on the paint. And the
acrylic must be wet. ~R

VODKA

GIN →

FINGERPRINTS

In this book cover, I used the bleach example I created on the previous pages, darkening the color in Photoshop. For the background I used a strip of one of my monoprints (see Chapter 13).
~C

With a bleach pen, you can totally eliminate someone from a photo, such as an ex-husband. Only a white shape will remain. Very handy.
~R

Bleach pen on photographs

Those bleach pens from the grocery store that don't work on watercolor can work perfectly great—in a funky way—on photographs. Just draw on the photo with the pen. Let it sit a few minutes, then wipe it away or wash it off under running water. This works on your old photos that were printed by a traditional photo processing shop, as well as those printed on photo paper from your own desktop color printer. *~R*

To get the layered effect shown below, John Tollett (the designer of these CD labels) first drew the initial shapes, wiped off the bleach, then drew over the same shapes to take out more color.

25 Tape and Paint

Tools and materials

- Watercolors or acrylic paints
- Watercolor paper, canvas, or other substrate
- Watercolor palette
- Water
- Brushes
- Archival masking tape or household masking tape

One technique that is simple but very interesting is to use masking tape as a stencil. Masking tape can be torn to give an appealing ragged edge. You can layer your washes over the tape to get a very clean but textural effect.

Tip! *Also check out the masking tape technique on page 55 for a bit grubbier look.*

~R

1 Start with a dry sheet of water-color paper. You can use an already painted surface, but make sure it's very dry.

2 Take pieces of low-tack archival crepe-paper masking tape and cut or tear them into shapes and strips. Affix them to the watercolor paper and make sure you rub the edges down tight.

(If you don't have or need archival tape, use plain ol' masking tape.)

3 Paint over the tapes and allow them to dry. You can repeat the process to get a very layered, interesting texture, as shown below.

Easy stripes, tape as resist

1 To make some great stripes for a surface, lightly lay down masking tape on a pre-painted surface.

2 Paint lightly over the page and the tape.

3 When it's dry, carefully peel up the masking tape. The edges might be a little funky, which is good!

4 If you want to blend the stripes into the background a bit, add a colored glaze (mix acrylic paint with glazing liquid or matte medium) and paint over the whole area.

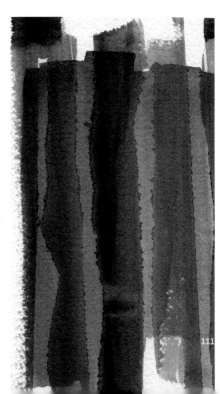

26 Plastic Wrap and Paint

Tools and materials

- Watercolors or acrylics
- Watercolor paper, canvas, or other substrate
- Paint palette
- Water
- Brushes
- Plastic wrap or plastic bag

This is one of the easiest of all the techniques to do, but it is also a favorite and delivers a very sophisticated, mottled result. It's quite amazing how many things you can find in your kitchen (or garage) that make perfect materials to use for water media effects.

You can easily do this with acrylic paints as well.

Using this technique with acrylic paint, I created a great night sky for a shadowbox illustration for The Shakespeare Papers. *~R*

1 Paint a heavy, juicy wash on a sheet of watercolor paper or canvas.

This technique works best when the color is on the darker side so the effect is more visible. Watercolor dries lighter than it looks when wet, so make sure you don't do anything too wimpy.

2 Take a piece of plastic wrap the size of your piece and place it over the wet wash.

 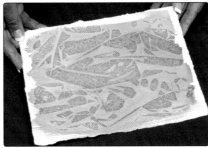

3 Mush the plastic wrap around in the paint and make sure you have lots of wrinkles all over the surface.

Let the piece air dry.

4 When it's dry, peel off the plastic wrap. It's always a pleasant surprise to see the texture.

Of course, immediately scan it to use in another interesting design.

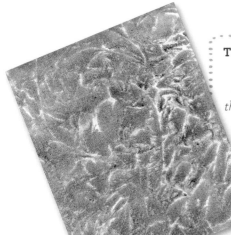

Tip! *If you don't have plastic wrap handy, grab any plastic bag. Poke it around in the wet paint, then peel it off even before it's dry. Or wait until it's dry for a crisper effect.* ~R

113

27 Paper Towels and Paint

Tools and materials

- Watercolor or acrylic paints
- Palette of some sort
- Water
- Brushes
- Paper towels with patterns on them
- Spritzer, if you have one
- Freezer paper or wax paper

Don't neglect the paper towels that are probably sitting in your kitchen or studio right now. The sturdy kind with embossed patterns have many uses! Once you've dyed them, as explained here, use them as backgrounds, in collages, in found-object art.

As you're working on any paint project, keep the paper towels with which you wipe up messes or rub off paint—spritz them and crinkle them up, then let them dry. *Voilà!* New art.

The embossed patterns act as great stamps, too—they quickly and easily apply texture to your paint.

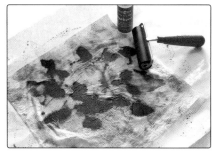

1 For a large overall pattern, lay a paper towel that has an embossed pattern onto your wet acrylic paint, lightly pat the towel with your hand so the pattern embeds into the paint, then pull it off.

2 While that towel is still wet with paint, use it as a stamp on another project or two!

1 Dye paper towels with watercolors or acrylics. Fold them up or roll them or tie them with string and dip parts of the towels into little bowls of watery color, similar to tie-dying a t-shirt.

2 Unfold the towel. If necessary, spritz it with water to mush the colors together.

1 On wax paper or the shiny side of freezer paper, paint with watery color or drizzle fluid acrylics. Lay a paper towel into the paint. Spritz it, brayer it, or rub it (or all three) until the towel is soaked with paint.

2 If there's a lot of paint on the towel, press or dab it onto another substrate (see the example on the opposite page).

3 If the paper towel is double-layered, pull apart the layers and you've got two sheets! The thinner sheets can be used like washi in the technique shown in Chapter 12.

Far left: *I used a paper towel to create the texture on the background of this illustration. I then added a layer of gel tinted with color and scratched into it for a slight illusion of rain.*

Near left: *The paper towel is actually the background, glued down with gel. I added a layer of tinted gel on top and scratched more texture into it.*

Combine Techniques!

Combine the possibilities! These pages have been washed, splattered, blown, and stamped. You can see leaves, metallic watercolors, stencils from the office supply store, and store-bought stamps. While you're throwing paint around, you might as well make a whole bunch of pages to keep in your files for future projects, including collage or found-object illustrations. Or cut them up into mosaic pieces. So much to do!

PART 4

Paper & Metal Projects

Paper is the basis of the graphic design industry. This section includes a number of techniques that are focused specifically on paper, including how to make your own.

And metal—who doesn't like a little bling? One has only to view the illuminated manuscripts dating back to classical antiquity to know that written words can be decorated as if they were fine jewels.

I like to incorporate a touch of metal in my work. I try to keep it under control—it can be quite tempting to slather everything in sight with metal leaf, shiny paint, or drips of gold. But if used thoughtfully, these techniques can add other layers and dimensions to your design work.

Paper & Metal

Play with this most physical symbol of design!

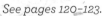

28 Marble the Paper

Hand marbling has been around for centuries. You only have to visit a shop that carries old books and look at their end papers to see the results of this ancient and beautiful technique.

See pages 120–123.

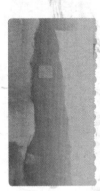
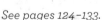

29 Collage with Paper

Collage building is creative and intriguing as you find bits and pieces and slowly embody your vision.

See pages 124–133.

30 Collage with Metal

Add an extra-special touch to your digital work with simple techniques for working with metal.

See pages 134–139.

31 Make your own Paper

Make your own paper! Embed it with particles that tie the background into the subject material you're working on. The interesting feathered edges and uneven opacities that appear when you make your own sheets add great depth to digital design work.

See pages 140–149.

32 Cast Paper 3D Images

While you've got your tub and blender out to make paper, also make some cast paper three-dimensional objects as design illustrations.

See pages 150–155.

33 Blind-Emboss the Paper

Simulate the expensive look of a blind emboss, where the image is not printed, but the paper is raised up instead, creating a subtle but tactile image.

See pages 156–159.

34 Gold-Stamp the Paper

Paint an embossed or debossed image with metal paint to simulate the look of a foil stamp.

See pages 160–161.

35 Metal-Leaf an Image

Use inexpensive metal leaf to simulate the look of gilt (gold leaf). Try it on letters, images, sculpted areas of a collage, and more.

See pages 162–163.

36 Emboss with Powders

With embossing powders and a heat gun, you can create handmade elements with a touch of elegance. This is an easy technique to add by hand to short-run projects.

See pages 164–167.

28 Marble the Paper

Tools and materials

- Methocel (methycellulose)
- Household ammonia (not the sudsy kind)
- Printmaking paper
- Alum powder (for preparing the paper)
- Acrylic paints made for marbling
- Versatex Dispersant or ox gall liquid (optional)
- Shallow vat for "heavy water"
- Paper towels
- Eye droppers
- Skewers and/or marbling combs

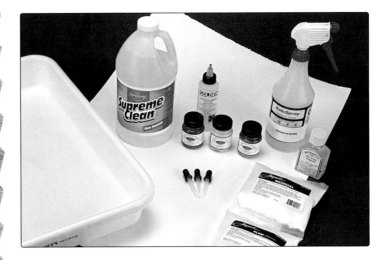

To marble paper, you'll float marbling paint on specially prepared water, then dip the paper onto that floating paint.

Traditional marbling can be a labor-intensive, smelly, and somewhat toxic process. Of course, traditional marbling provides the most stunning results, but I don't have the time, facilities, or odor stamina to deal with it, so I use a kinder, gentler approach.

If we put paint, even oil paint, on top of regular water, the paint quickly sinks. In traditional marbling, a material called carrageenan moss (an edible seaweed) is boiled and allowed to cure; this creates "heavy water." The paint sits on top of this heavy water long enough for us to create a design and transfer it to paper.

Unfortunately, this wonderful carrageenan moss gives off the smell of rotting eggs. I can only do so much for art—consequently, I use a synthetic material, Methocel, to create my heavy water. I also find oil paints too messy (even for me), so I use specially formulated acrylic marbling inks that give very satisfactory results.

Light BFK printmaking paper works well as a substrate because it has no texture to speak of and can withstand the numerous applications of water inherent in the marbling process.

Before marbling, you'll first create heavy water and prepare your paper and paint.

are the water:

about 1 to 1.5 ounces of Methocel with one gallon of room-temperature water in a large, flat pan.

2   Add one tablespoon of ammonia (not sudsy ammonia) and allow it to sit for about twenty minutes.

●   While your heavy water is setting up, prepare your paper to accept the marbling (see the next page).

—continued

Marbels

Toys and crafts for today's kids

5 Prepare the paint:
You must thin the marbling paint just so—it should be like half 'n' half cream. If the paint is not the right consistency, it will not sit on top of the heavy water properly but will sink to the bottom of the pan.

To help the paint float, you can mix a drop or two of Versatex Dispersant or ox gall into it.

3 Prepare the paper:
Make a solution of one tablespoon of alum powder to a quart of warm water; spray the side of the paper that you are going to dip into the paint. This makes the paper absorb less water (and thus more paint).

4 Allow the sheet of paper to dry while you prepare your paint. You can use a blow dryer to speed the drying.

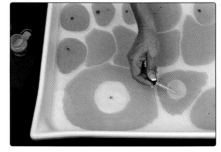

6 Add paint to the water:
Use an eye dropper to create a design on the top of the water by carefully dropping small amounts of the thinned acrylic paint.

Be careful to drop the paint while the dropper tip is close to the surface of the water so gravity doesn't pull most of your color to the bottom of the pan. The paint will spread into circles.

7 The first colors will disperse themselves into donut shapes. Now start filling the circles with another color.

When I visited Venice, I was enthralled with the absolutely gorgeous marbled papers available in the paper shops. The colors and patterns were as old as the cobblestones. Of course, being the cosista, I wanted to bring them all home for my collections. I did manage to sneak three sheets home and continue to use them for inspiration as I marble my own pages.

~C

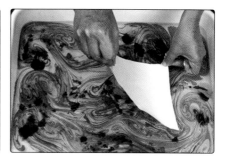

8 You want the surface to be full of color, so continue dropping paint onto the heavy water until you have a very colorful pan.

9 When you have enough color on the pan, take a skewer, stick, marblizing comb, or other tool and swirl the design on the heavy water.

10 **Dip your paper:** Take your dry sheet of paper. Hold it carefully and dip the alum-coated side onto the very surface of the water—corner to corner.

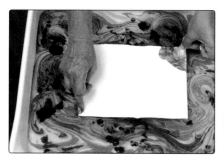
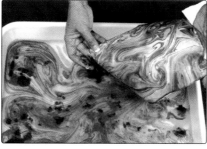

11 Make sure the paper is in contact with the surface and the color.

12 Pull up the paper quickly and rinse off the slimy residue with cool water—hold it under gently running cool water. Don't use a hard sprayer as it will ruin the marbling.

13 **Done!** Hang up your sheet of paper to dry like laundry, or speed up the process with your hair dryer.

Tip! Sometimes the dried sheet warps a little. This usually isn't a problem, but if you want it totally flat, spray the back of the sheet lightly with water, set it between two pieces of scrap paper, and put heavy books on it overnight.

29 Collage with Paper

Tools and materials

- Collection of copyright-free images
- Substrate
- UHU Tac temporary adhesive
  or Spray Mount,
  or Yes! Paste,
  or StudioTac sheets
- Cutting mat
- X-acto knife
- Metal cutting edge
- Paper scissors
- Burnisher

The tools and materials used for collage include those used by fine artists and illustrators, as well as those used by crafters and scrapbookers. And you get to play with unorthodox materials that produce stained marks or blanched areas.

On the paper that you plan to use in your collages, experiment with taking it a step beyond normal; create effects with bleach, shoe polish, markers, pastels, colored pencils, color crayons, inks, and other materials. Develop your own techniques with unusual surfaces and feel free to trash/destroy/embellish the different pieces.

Materials for Collage

You can collect and store a wide range of papers and other materials for use in collage. I'm always on the lookout for little scraps and pieces to use. I cut textures from magazines and look for unusual papers wherever I go. I buy old music scores, maps, receipts from antique stores. I love joss paper from Asian markets. Even the confetti in the Disneyland parade did not escape my acquisitive collage-aficionado notice. I keep everything organized and labeled in a portable file so I have what I need when inspiration strikes.

You don't need much to do collage: papers, a good cutting mat (see page 127), a metal straight edge, cutting tools, a brush, some glue, and something to paste everything onto. Most of all, you need a creative, experimental, and enthusiastic attitude.

Copyright issues

Obviously, as a collage illustrator, you don't want to end up in jail on copyright infringement charges, so you must be very careful not to "borrow" other people's stuff. If you are a student working on class projects, this is not so much of an issue because you are not publishing and making money on your student projects (and you probably aren't given a budget for buying photography and other art). However, as a practicing professional, you must pay for any photographs or other imagery—unless you find public domain and copyright-free sources. Make it a practice to be careful what you use in your collage illustrations.

Keep an eye out for all kinds of paper possibilities.

And see the appendix for sources for free and inexpensive images you can work with.

As a designer, I have always loved collage! It seems so modern, so direct, and very cool. I fell in love with Kurt Schwitters' work the first time I ever saw his beautiful pieces from the 1930s. Many of my favorite illustrators are collage artists. I love the textures, torn edges, rough cuts, ephemera with type on them, photographs — all the stuff collage artists use to create their pieces.

Of course, Photoshop is a wonderful tool for creating photomontages. It has capabilities that are not available to the hands-on artist, such as transparency effects. Nonetheless, there is a case to be made for getting out the art materials and chopping, tearing, spattering, gluing, and painting. The look can be perfect, gritty, dirty, messy, tidy, but always very human. ~C

Robin makes piles.

Creating papers for collage

You can create many of your own papers by coloring them yourself. Watercolors and acrylics are great media for coloring and creating textures on a variety of papers, as you can see by the multitude of techniques in this book.

One of the great things about painting your own patterns on watercolor paper is that you can get beautiful, white torn edges that provide a lot of contrast and texture to your illustration.

Experiment with splattering paints, inks, metallic markers, and opaque paint markers.

Rub charcoal, pastels, colored pencils, or "Distress Ink" stamp pads on scraps of paper or textures you've created to make your own special materials.

Be sure to save scraps from all projects! Even little pieces are very useful to the collage artist. I keep the little scraps in labeled envelopes.

Carmen creates neatly labeled envelopes.

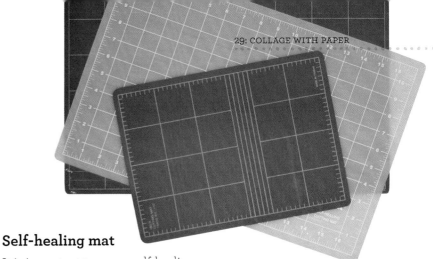

Substrates for collage

In addition to your found, created, or purchased papers, you need supports to affix the items on. You can use just about anything—wood, metal, canvas, watercolor paper, boxes, etc. Just make sure you use the appropriate adhesive for that substrate (see the following page).

Cutting tools

Due to the scrapbooking phenomenon, there are a lot of new gadgets for cutting on the market. There are sleek trimmers with fancy alternative blades. There are die-cutting devices that can cut perfect circles, squares, and other fancy shapes, and even handfuls of scissors with zig-zaggy blades (see pages 22–25). Many of these tools are useful to the designer for collage; however, don't get cutesy when you're creating serious illustration pieces.

Also, consider the cost. How often will you really use that snowflake punch for a significant collage illustration? Personally, I stick to simple geometrics and tools that are somewhat flexible (e.g., a tool that allows me to cut different circumferences of circles). Nonetheless, many of these crafter tools are perfect for graphic design applications, not only for digital design work, but also for creating 3D mockups to show a client or for a short run of handmade invitations, so I am always on the lookout for the latest and greatest cutting gadget.

Self-healing mat

It is important to own a self-healing mat to cut on. These indispensable devices can be purchased in a variety of sizes and colors. Many novice designers use the cardboard backs of art paper pads to cut on. "Hey, money saved," they mistakenly think! However, if you have ever spent several hours on an illustration and are ready to mount your masterpiece only to have your knife stick in a previous cut on the back of your cardboard pad and give you a crooked edge, you will appreciate the benefits of a self-healing mat.

I prefer the transparent mat because I can put it on my light table and see through it. I have several sizes— a very large one for big projects, a medium-sized one I can carry easily with me, and a tiny one that fits in my little graphic design kit that I carry whenever I travel.

Adhesives for Collage

There are a wide variety of glues and adhesives you can use for collage. You need to experiment and make sure to choose one that will work for your particular project. You may need more than one type of adhesive if you're using a variety of items.

Xyron Creative Station

For paper

Thin paper works well with an acrylic medium (such as your bottle of matte medium, polymer medium, or any of the gels) or Yes! Paste. Sobo and Elmer's white glues (polyvinyl acetates, aka PVA, aka polymers) can also be used.

Rubber cement

If you decide to use that old favorite paper glue—rubber cement—make sure you purchase an archival variety so your papers won't discolor over time.

For tiny pieces

I personally love a rub-down adhesive called StudioTac because it is a dry adhesive and I can use it on little bits of materials without glue oozing out all over the place and making a gooey mess.

For heavier items

Heavier items need stronger adhesives. Wood and metallics might need epoxy glues, E-6000, or acrylic modeling paste.

Gadgets for gluing

The scrapbooking industry has come out with all sorts of adhesive application gadgets that can be a little bit pricey, but oh so cool and oh so tidy. I have the Xyron 900 (about $80) that puts a nice thin coat of adhesive on the backs of my papers with a couple turns of a little handle.

Temporary adhesives

UHU Tac or other poster putties are great temporary adhesives to use with collage for those times when you want to put pieces in place just to see how they look.

Spray adhesives

Spray adhesives work very well with collage. They give a very fine mist to the back of the item, which means you will avoid unsightly bumps and oozing edges when you affix your piece to a flat substrate.

Be sure to always spray your items outside or in a spray booth (a big box makes a cheap, temporary spray booth); minute particles of glue are released into the air when you spray and then descend to coat not only your artwork, but also your carpet, your cat, and unsuspecting toddlers. Before long

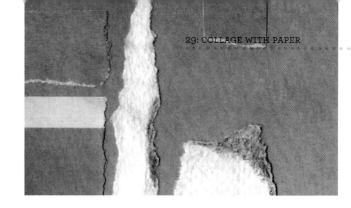

there will be a dirty spot on your floor, the cat will be festooned with dust bunnies, and your toddler will have Cheerios stuck to his shoulders. If spraying outside, always put a sheet of newspaper down to protect your sidewalk or garage floor or you will have ugly markings where the dirt sticks to the overspray.

There are a variety of spray adhesives you can purchase. Some are strong enough to glue down your carpet, like Super 77. Others have very low tack (stickiness) and can be used for temporary positioning. As a design professional, you will probably need a can of each.

Spray adhesives are not cheap! Protect your investment by keeping your nozzle very clean. When you are done coating your artwork, turn the can upside-down, put a paper towel in front of the nozzle, and give a couple squirts. Wipe off the nozzle carefully. If your nozzle does become clogged, get a new one from your art supply store, or try and clean the hole with a Q-tip and some rubber cement thinner or fingernail polish remover.

Burnishing

Once you are finished with your collage, it's a good idea to make sure everything is stuck down firmly before you scan your masterpiece. See page 25 for examples of burnishers that will come in handy.

Be efficient!

As designer, it's important to use efficient tools and methods to develop your digital design work and to make sure you're creating appropriate visual communication. Sure, you can fix a lot of stuff in Photoshop, but is that the best use of your time? If you are careful from the beginning and do a tidy, clean, thorough job, you can avoid that tedious repair work in your digital imaging application.

Although keep in mind that we have that great advantage as digital designers—if necessary, we *can* fix things! We're not making wall art! It's extraordinarily liberating.

~R

 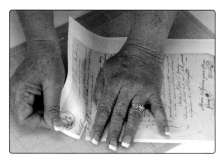

1   After you have decided what you want to say with your collage, choose your materials and start laying them out.

Sometimes a free and direct approach creates the best solution. Other times, especially if your collage piece is being directed by a specific project, it's important to start the illustration by creating thumbnail ideas that will fit the format and goals of the piece. You, the designer, must choose the most efficient and effective approach given the parameters of your final project.

2   After selecting some initial pieces of paper, textures, photographs, ephemera, etc., start arranging them, cutting them, tearing them, drawing on them until the design takes form and starts to communicate your message effectively.

You may find as you start laying out your elements that you need to either make more pieces, find more pieces, or buy more pieces. This is the way it works, so go with the flow and be flexible. Do what you need to do.

Tip! *Think about the proportions of your project. Your illustrations or text must fit into a specific format, so it is important to design appropriately. It is often easier to build the collage a little larger than you'll need it and reduce the image in the computer. However, it's difficult to make a long, rectangular image or block of text fit into a square format, so at least create your parameters proportionately from the get-go.*

3   Put down some large shapes to anchor the collage. Remember that contrast is your friend, so vary the edges, relative sizes, colors, and textures for a more dynamic and effective piece.

4   Taking elements out can be as important as putting them in, so don't be afraid to take elements out if they compromise your vision.

5   It's a good idea to put your collage together temporarily for the first round of concepts—clients are notorious for changing their minds. I like to use tiny little balls of poster putty to make my elements stay in place for my first scan.

6   Once your client has approved the basic collage (if that's necessary), it's time to put it together.

One of my favorite adhesives is Yes! Paste, but it must be spread on your papers very smoothly and evenly. I use a little spreader I got at the hardware store (shown above), but you could just as easily use a clean-cut piece of mat board.

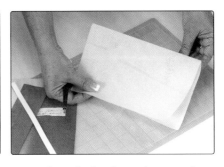

7   I also like to use Letraset StudioTac for small pieces. This is a rub-on transfer adhesive. StudioTac is basically little dots of sticky stuff that are affixed to a translucent sheet of material. To use it, first peel off the backing sheet that protects the adhesive.

8   Rub the sticky dots onto your piece of material with a burnisher, then rub your piece onto the collage.

9   Replace the backing sheet on the StudioTac.

—continued

10 Burnish your elements onto your collage. I like using the low-tack variety of StudioTac because I sometimes want to make minor adjustments and low tack material allows some flexibility.

11 Another favorite collage adhesive is matte medium (shown above). It goes on smoothly and dries totally clear with a matte finish.

When scanning, we want to avoid shiny stuff because reflective materials can cause hot spots on your image. Remember, we are trying to avoid having to retouch in Photoshop.

Do a tidy, precise job of putting your collage together. Keep your fingers clean, and try to avoid glues that are too liquid.

When your piece is finished, take a clean sheet of tissue paper, lay it over the collage, and burnish everything into place.

After I finished and scanned the collage, I continued the collage process in the computer, as you can see above.

*A mystery student left this intriguing collage in the trash.
Of course I couldn't toss it—it's found art! And beautifully done.*

*As you can see, the textures from magazines, numbers from
an old receipt, and a piece of washi paper with chunks of
newspaper embedded make for a unique composition.*

*The lesson here: Never toss what you might think of as less-
than-successful (or an enterprising colleague just might dig
it out of the trash and use it for an interesting poster).*

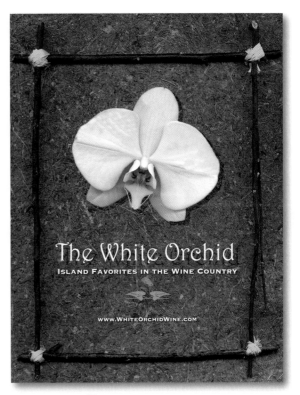

Scanner collage

I built my own little scanner darkroom for scanning
3D objects. It's just a little box out of black foam
board and black photographer's tape, 2 inches deep,
that fits right inside the glass frame of my scanner.

I fastened the fresh orchid (shown above) to the
inside of the black box with UHU Tac and scanned
it; if I had put the flower directly on the glass, it
would have smashed the delicate petals.

I built the frame with willow sticks and raffia,
affixed it to a piece of bark paper with UHU Tac,
and scanned that as well.

In Photoshop, I combined the scans, then added
the text in InDesign.

30 Collage with Metal

Tools and materials

- Substrate: canvas, watercolor paper, Bristol board, etc.
- Sheet of art metal (I used copper)
- Copper topper (I used Sophisticated Finishes Copper Metallic Surfacer)
- Patina
- Hole punches
- Grommets (eyelets), grommet setting tool, and pad
- Burnisher with stylus tip
- Metal ruler
- Brush
- Paper piecer
- Cutting mat
- Wire brush
- Masking tape

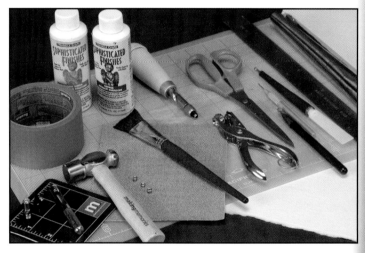

Collage can include all types of materials, including metals and grommets (metal eyelets, little round things, that get inserted into holes to finish the edges). Sheets of art metal are in most hobby and art stores. You can cut it into specific shapes, distress the surface, and even emboss words and designs into it. Your project won't be exactly like this one, but if you follow along, you'll learn several tips and techniques that will help in creating your own metal work.

If you decide to work with sheets of art metal, be aware that they have very sharp edges. I highly recommend you wear gloves when you cut and bend the metal.

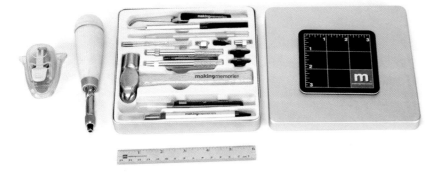

One of my favorite tool sets comes in handy for this kind of project—a delightful little box for the paper artist from Making Memories. I have the deluxe set, which costs about $40 and comes packed in a lovely tin case. It has a craft knife, glue pen, hammer, hole punch with three head sizes, universal eyelet (grommet) setter, four different heads, tweezers, set of four needles, paper piercer deluxe, stylus, 6" ruler, and a black setting mat. Now you know what to ask for on Valentines Day!

As an alternative to grommets (eyelets), there is a huge selection of beautiful metal brads in the hobby stores. All you need is something to poke a hole in the metal, then use the brads to attach the metal to the rest of the collage.

And don't limit yourself to using these with metal—incorporate these lovely brads into any collage. ~R

1 For this collage, I'm going to use a variety of metallic effects. I've already created a patina (see Chapter 8) on a piece of this collage and now I'm going to create a pattern for a piece of art metal I want to incorporate.

On a piece of vellum, draw the shape that you want to be metal.

2 Cut out the shape carefully, allowing an extra ½" all the way around because you need to fold the metal under by at least that much to get rid of the sharp edges.

3 Cut a piece of thin art metal off the roll with a pair of old scissors that you have designated for such tasks, or use tin snips. Don't use your newest pair of precision scissors because cutting metal will dull the blades.

—continued

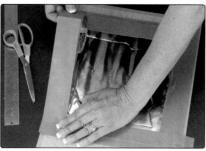

4 Trace your pattern onto your piece of metal with a pencil. Press firmly and make an indentation you will be able to follow.

5 If you want to inscribe the metal, place it over something with a little give, such as those thin foam pads from the craft store (metal crafters use pads made of suede). I've placed mine over a cutting mat.

Tape all around your piece of metal so it doesn't move and—more importantly—so you don't cut yourself on the sharp edges.

6 Use an embossing stylus and draw firmly into the metal (choose a fine tip for delicate lines, a larger tip for deeper, chunkier lines).

7 Take off the tape and cut out the shape. Be careful not to slice your fingers. Really, you should be wearing gloves.

8 Clip the corners ½" inch diagonally toward the center.

9 Fold the edge over towards the back. With your burnishing tool, rub down the edge on the back side.

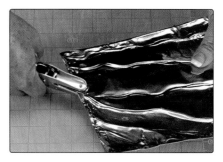

10 Turn the piece over and rub down the edge with your burnishing tool on the front as well.

11 I plan to fasten my piece to the collage with grommets, plus I want a pattern of holes around the edge for embellishment, so I mark where I want the holes to go.

12 Using my hole punch, I punch out the holes. On the thick corners, I'll use Martha Stewart's screw punch, a handy tool for your collection.

13 I want to distress the surface, so I'm beating it up with a piece of fine-grit sandpaper and using a wire brush to scrape it.

—continued

14 To attach the metal to the collage with grommets, first make marks in the hole centers with a needle, probe, or awl.

15 Place a little punching mat (one comes in the tool kit) or a piece of scrap wood under the area where you are going to punch.

16 With my hole punch, I can use a hammer. I punch out the holes in my substrate.

17 Pop the grommet in the hole.

18 Turn your collage over and set the grommet so it doesn't pop out. Now carry on and finish your collage!

I applied a patina to the metal, as explained in Chapter 8.

I wanted kind of a gritty look in this poster, and the punched metal gave me some of that. I also wanted to capture the colors and textures of the rocks, foliage, and sands that are part of Rio de Janeiro's landscape. I used modeling pastes, gels with inclusions, patinas, sanding, even a little gold embossing, along with acrylic paints to get a layered effect.

~C

I set the type in InDesign, printed it, taped it to the copper, then embossed the text by hand into the metal from the back side.

~R

31 Make your own Paper

Tools and materials

- Cotton linters or papers
- Large plastic tub
- Blender
- Papermaking screen (wooden frame with screen attached) and deckle (empty wooden frame)
- Shallow tray larger than papermaking screen
- Piece of plastic window screen same size as deckle
- White craft felts
- White tea towels or cotton napkins
- Press bar or a clean household sponge
- Household iron

  (or use a papermaking kit from ArnoldGrummer.com or a craft store)

Papermaking is a simple process that has so many possibilities for the graphic designer. The beautiful feathery edges that you get, called deckle edges (the hallmark of handmade papers) are one reason I like making my own paper.

You can also put a variety of elements right into the paper pulp to create perfect background textures for many graphic design pieces. I am always finding new things that can be mixed in the pulp for interesting effects.

Although this process looks like a lot of trouble, it actually takes a lot less time than you'd think. And it is extremely satisfying.

1 Fill a plastic tub (large enough to put your papermaking screen in) half full with warm water.

Fill a blender to the four-cup mark with warm water.

2 If you're using recycled paper, tear it up into small pieces and put a large handful in the blender. If you have purchased whole sheets of cotton linter, tear up the sheet into small pieces. (If you want to use old rags, first see pages 146–147.)

Note: *Don't ever put long strips of paper in the blender because they will wrap around the blades and burn out the blender engine.* Be careful! My darling students have caused the sad end of several machines this way. And be sure to use plenty of water.

—continued

These linters (which look like heavy lint) create a very white paper, just aching for some color or inclusions. These are also terrific for paper casting—see the next chapter.

I sometimes use already chopped up paper linters from the Arnold Grummer line of materials at the art or craft store.

If you want to recycle, use junk mail or paper around the house. Just remember that whatever you use for pulp will determine the color and finish of your sheet of paper. If you choose paper that has been printed, the printing inks will give the paper a mucky, gray, industrial tone.

If you plan to write on your sheet of paper or keep it around for posterity, add ⅛ of a teaspoon of Acid pHree or Paper Additive into your blender. It has calcium carbonate, which acts as a filler to give your paper a smoother surface, and it also neutralizes the acids that deteriorate paper.

141

3 Whiz the paper in the blender thoroughly. You usually want a fine-grade pulp—the finer the pulp, the smoother the paper. (And the more pulp you put in the tub, the thicker the paper.)

4 Pour the pulp into your large plastic tub of warm water. Depending on the size of your tub, it will probably take more than one blender full of pulp to get the right proportion of pulp to water. My eight-gallon tub takes three or four blenders full of pulp.

 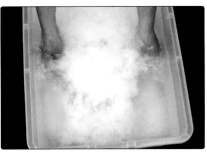

5 Swish the paper pulp around with your hand until the pulp and water are thoroughly mixed.

Hold your papermaking screen vertically, screen side towards you, and plunge it vertically into the plastic tub of pulp. Do this with as little wiggling and movement as possible. Smooth, graceful, quiet hands make better, even sheets of paper.

6 When you hit the bottom of the tub, turn the papermaking screen horizontal—screen side facing up.

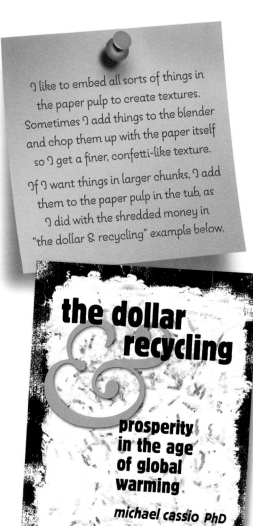

I like to embed all sorts of things in the paper pulp to create textures. Sometimes I add things to the blender and chop them up with the paper itself so I get a finer, confetti-like texture.

If I want things in larger chunks, I add them to the paper pulp in the tub, as I did with the shredded money in "the dollar & recycling" example below.

the dollar & recycling

prosperity in the age of global warming

michael cassio PhD

7 Pull the screen straight up with one deliberate motion. You want the pulp evenly distributed on the screen, so if it's lumpy or thin on one edge, dump the pulp off your screen, stir it gently, and try the process again.

8 Put your papermaking screen into an empty tray to catch all the dripping water. Put the empty wooden frame (the deckle) on top of your pulp. Match it up with the sides of the paper screen and press hard; this creates that lovely feathered (deckled) edge.

  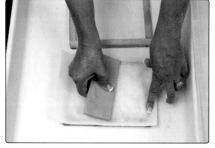

9 Carefully remove the deckle without disturbing the paper pulp.

10 Put a piece of window screen on top of your paper pulp.

11 Using a press bar (if you have one, shown above, perhaps from a papermaking kit) or a book wrapped in a plastic bag or a clean household sponge, press the water out of your sheet of paper.

Press hard. You want to get out as much water as you can. However, you don't want the screen to move, so hold it firmly in place as you press the water out with your free hand.

— continued

143

12 After you've gotten out as much water as you can, wipe the water out of your big tray with a towel.

Gently peel off the window screen and set it aside.

13 Put a piece of white craft felt (or clean pieces of an old sheet) in the bottom of the dry tray.

14 Turn over your papermaking screen and put it down on the white felt, paper-pulp–side down. The paper pulp should be in contact with the felt.

15 Using a press bar or clean household sponge, press out more water. This is called "couching" the paper (pronounced "kooching").

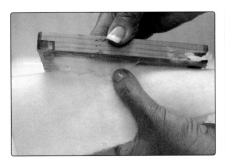

16 Pick up the felt and screen. Using a fingernail, tease a corner of the paper pulp off the screen. This usually works to start releasing the sheet of paper from the papermaking screen.

17 Gently dump the sheet of paper onto a dry felt or a piece of an old sheet.

18 Now you can iron your sheet of paper (on the "cotton" setting) between pressing cloths or tea towels. Or hang it up to dry, or lay it on a clean, flat surface to dry naturally.

Remember, "mistakes" often make interesting pieces, so experiment! Most of the time you are not going to make pages that need to be uniform. So if your sheet is a little wobbly, don't worry too much—you might be tearing it up for a collage anyway.

~C

Your sheet of paper

Your first handmade sheet of paper can be so exciting!

Now what to do with it? First, before you do anything with it at all—scan it. At a high resolution. Now you have a digital file of your paper that you can use over and over again. If you want to collage with this piece, you can tear it up but still have the digital image available for something like, say, a wine label.

In this Marletta wine label example, I scanned the handmade paper with a sheet of black paper over the back of it so the feather edge showed up beautifully. If the back of your scanner lid is white (mine is), you know that when you scan white pieces, it's difficult to separate them from the background.

I touched up a couple of little areas of the paper in Photoshop, placed the TIFF image in InDesign, and set my type. To die-cut this label into the shape of the ragged edge of the paper would be formidably expensive, so I put the label on a black background to blend in with the full bottle of wine.

This (above) is made from an old gingham cotton napkin, the last one from a set that my children grew up with (see the following pages about making paper from old rags). I put pieces of an old sheet beneath and above the paper, some twine directly beneath the paper, and set bricks on top to press it dry. I'm sure, as a designer, you can imagine the possibilities of pressing shapes into your handmade paper. Use cardboard shapes, thick stencils, natural objects, etc. ~R

Papermaking with rags

I'd never made paper before reading Carmen's instructions here, and I was intrigued to see if I could make paper from cotton and linen rags, old clothes and napkins. I discovered there was just one extra step in the process, shown below. ~*R*

You'll need:

- **Cotton or linen rags**
- **A non-aluminum cooking pot**
- **Baking soda**
- **Strainer**

Before following Carmen's directions starting from Step 1 (pages 141–145), first do this:

1 Cut up some old linen or cotton item into tiny pieces. Do not use wool or synthetic fabrics!

If you are using new fabric fresh from the fabric store, be sure to wash it first to remove the sizing.

In this example, I'm using a leg from a pair of well-worn and well-loved linen pants that were falling apart but I just couldn't bear to throw them away. Thank goodness I didn't.

Use good sharp scissors to cut the fabric into tiny pieces.

2 Put the fabric in a non-aluminum pot with plenty of water.

Add a few spoonfuls of baking soda.

Let it simmer at a low boil for at least an hour. Keep an eye on it because it will boil over, as you can see above. Don't worry—it cleans up easily.

Fiskars fabric scissors make short work of cutting up the fabric, but be careful with them—I'm still missing a fingerprint that my Fiskars removed when I was 15 years old and snipped a piece of thread; the Fiskars took my fingerprint off my finger as easily as it snipped the thread.

~R

I have a book press because I'm learning to bookbind. I discovered it makes a great paper press as well. I put various objects under the damp paper sheets and pressed them between paper towels and old bed sheets to create impressions in the paper. You can always use bricks or heavy books instead of a press. ~*R*

3 Rinse the soggy fabric through a strainer. Rinse it well to get out all the baking soda.

4 Now go to page 141 and follow Carmen's directions for making your own paper.

Make sure you put plenty of water and not too much fabric in the blender at a time—fabric is sturdier than paper and the extra work the blender has to go through can burn out the motor. Guess how I discovered that interesting tidbit.

Paper made with cotton or linen is archival—it's 100 percent *rag* paper. Paper made with wood pulp disintegrates when wet; rag paper doesn't (which is why your dollar bills go through the laundry just fine).

Wood pulp paper wasn't invented until the mid-1800s in Canada and Germany, which is why we still have such a large collection of really old manuscripts and books—everything they used to write and print on (including parchment and vellum from animal skins) was archival quality!

In 1660 in England, a law was passed making it illegal to be buried in cotton or linen; you had to be buried in wool because you can't make paper out of wool. This saved 200,000 pounds of fabric a year that was then available for papermaking.

~*R*

I cut out a stencil (with my nifty hot-tip stencil cutter-outer, as shown on page 159) and placed it under a damp sheet of my new linen paper. It turns out that impressed shapes appear better on light-colored sheets. So I used a gold leafing pen and colored in the barely visible imprint from the stencil, as shown above.

Inclusions

In this example I mixed in pieces of bark with the paper pulp. These added elements are called "inclusions." You can put all kinds of things in your paper pulp—dried flowers, bits of glitter, pieces of metal leaf, small cuttings of threads and strings, confetti—anything as long as it is dry. You don't want your paper to mold, so fresh plants and flowers won't work very well.

My talented student, Nichole Coggiola, gave me this lovely sheet of paper with bark inclusions; I scanned the whole sheet because I love the edges. I used my photograph of a Boca musician and gave it a warm sepia tone in Photoshop, using the Hue/Saturation palette (click the Colorize button and adjust the tones). In InDesign, I used the eyedropper tool to sample colors out of the sheet of paper and photograph for the typography. I like to tie the images and backgrounds together for unity and elegance. ~C

In this collage, I bought the piece of washi paper with the chunks of newspaper already embedded in it (you don't have to make EVERYTHING yourself). I combined that with my own pressed leaves and other elements for this piece on recyling. ~C

148

Fiber paste (fake handmade paper)

In a hurry, but you really want a handmade paper look? Grab a jar of fiber paste from the art store. If you want a slight color to it, add a touch of acrylic paint. ~R

1 Using a spatula or putty knife, spread a thin layer of fiber paste on a piece of wax paper or freezer paper.

2 Mush the edges with your fingers to give a semblance of a deckle edge.

3 Let it dry.

4 Peel it up.

Once you create the "paper," you can paint on it, print on it, tear it, cut it, use it in a collage, etc. It's not nearly as amazingly wonderful as your own paper, but it has one advantage— because it's not made with wood pulp, it won't disintegrate when wet.

I tinted a small bowl of the fiber paste and added the leftover bits of wood shavings from my wood carving to make this fake paper.

I painted this piece with clear Digital Ground (see page 19), taped the top and several inches down the side to a piece of regular bond paper, and put it through my cheap ink jet printer. Now it's ready to use in a project.

149

32 Cast Paper 3D Images

Tools and materials

- Item to cast
- Paper linters
- Blender
- Plastic tub
- Sculpey clay
- Pasta maker (optional)
- Pam cooking spray (optional)
- Aluminum foil
- Baking plate
- Parchment baking paper

Cast paper is a wonderful technique for creating 3D illustrations.

To make cast paper you need a mold. Many people use plaster of Paris to make molds, but that means buying big bags of powdery, dusty stuff and mixing it with water, lathering your casting item in petroleum jelly, pouring the sloppy wet stuff over your casting item while making sure you have appropriate seams so you can take your mold apart, waiting for the whole thing to dry . . . I don't have time for the process or the mess, so I use my handy-dandy Sculpey clay to make molds. I've even picked leaves from outside my husband's office and made cast paper pieces with the leaves and Sculpey.

Find or make something you want to cast in paper. All kinds of things can be cast—bark, rocks, spoons, tooth molds from the dentist, bowls, leaves, your child's plaster-of-Paris handprint, etc. Of course, your object should have something to do with your graphic design project.

You need to have a blender full of paper pulp—see pages 141–142 for this process. And hey, if you're making a tub full of pulp, you might as well make your own paper at the same time!

1   Here I have chosen a large shell that will make an interesting shape in cast paper.

If you are making your own clay mold with tools (instead of covering an existing object), make it and then skip to Step 6 to bake your clay. The mold doesn't need to be very deep at all.

2   Cover your object with aluminum foil. Rub the foil down thoroughly so you can pick up all the nuances of the shape you have chosen. If you want to make doubly sure the clay will pop off the foil, spray the foiled shape with Pam.

3   Roll out the Sculpey quite thin using the smallest setting on your dependable pasta maker (see page 187 about pasta makers for clay).

If you don't have a pasta maker, roll it out as thin as you can.

4   Cover your object with the Sculpey, making sure *not* to wrap the clay underneath the edges. You want to be able to just pop the object out of the mold easily and not break it in the process.

5   Smooth the clay down hard—you want to pick up as much detail from the object as you can.

—continued

6   Once the object is covered with the thin clay, set it on a parchment-lined cookie sheet or baking pan and bake it in the oven at 250 for about 20 minutes (if you used a different brand of polymer clay, check the baking directions!).

7   After the clay has cooled, carefully pop the clay mold off the foil-covered object.

8   Get your blender of paper pulp (see page 141) and scoop the pulp into the mold, patting it down with your fingers. Make sure no pulp is wrapped around the edges of your mold because you want the shape to pop out easily.

9   Once you have filled the mold, press out as much water as you can.

10 Turn your oven down as low as it will go and put your pulp-filled mold back onto the parchment-covered cookie sheet and back in the oven. Make sure you place the mold with the pulp face-up so it will meld itself into the shape.

It may take up to eight hours to totally dry, depending on how thick the pulp is.

11 Once it is totally dry, carefully loosen the paper shape and pop it out of the mold.

Now you have a lovely facsimile of the original shape. Use it in a 3D assemblage, paint it, color it, embellish it.

If you're careful throughout this process, you can use your mold again to create another piece.

In this cast paper illustration, I used a lot of other techniques along with my cast paper shell.

For the background, I painted the sky and sand with watercolor washes, then flicked a few grains of salt in the sand for texture (Chapter 15). Notice how even that little bit of texture entices your eye down to the name of the author.

For the center swath, I found a piece of heavily textured paper and painted it with a warm copper acrylic.

Where the textured paper meets the sand, I applied a strip of absorbent ground (Chapter 12), which I then painted with watercolors.

I scanned this entire background.

I then took my feather-light paper shell, painted it with red basecoat, leafed it with gold metal leafing (Chapter 35), then finished it off with a patina (Chapter 8).

I affixed my shell in my little scanner box (page 133) with UHU Tac and scanned it.

I put the shell and background scans together in Photoshop, then placed the flattened TIFF in InDesign, where I finished it up with the type.

I made this cast-paper shape using a fancy cookie mold, then ripped it in half. You can also see the pattern of lines bleached into paper (Chapter 24), the red handmade washi paper that I bought (page 60), and the marbled paper I made (Chapter 28).

Too much work?

You might think this seems like an awful lot of work for one project! But remember, **you** are a *digital* artist, so once you start collecting your handmade elements, you can reuse them in a variety of projects. Change the color of the handmade paper, resize and reverse the marbled textures, scan the bleached lines at a huge size so you see the paper weave. Never think that all the work you're doing will only go into one project!

And if you buy a bag of cotton linters (see page 141), you can be making paper casts in minutes.

Using old wooden type, I made molds of the letters in polymer clay, baked the molds, and then made the cast paper letters. **~R**

154

Cast paper with rag pulp

You can, of course, use your paper pulp that you made from cotton or linen rags, as explained on pages 146–147. Or try dryer lint from cotton or linen items. ~*R*

I had an old yellow gingham napkin that was the last of a set my kids grew up on. I just couldn't throw it away, which is a terrific thing because I followed Carmen's directions for cast paper and made this beautiful piece with it (yes, this is the same napkin in the paper on page 145).

I used a fancy baking pan as a mold. I don't know yet what kind of design project I'll use it in, but I'm sure the perfect thing will appear.

This didn't take as long as you might think. I cut up the napkin into bits and put it in the pot with baking soda to boil. Rinsed it, blended it, and mushed it into the mold. Sponged out the water and let it dry. Voilà! I did it while I putzed around cleaning the kitchen.

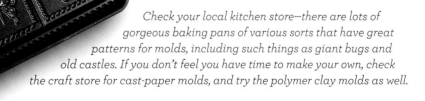

Check your local kitchen store—there are lots of gorgeous baking pans of various sorts that have great patterns for molds, including such things as giant bugs and old castles. If you don't feel you have time to make your own, check the craft store for cast-paper molds, and try the polymer clay molds as well.

155

33 Blind-Emboss the Paper

Tools and materials

- Image to blind emboss
- Stencil material
- Embossing stylus
- X-acto knife
  with new blade
- Lightbox

The embossed effect—raised letters or image on paper—is irresistible. But most of our clients can't afford embossing; it's a special printing technique that is only used on high-end jobs, such as wine labels, special presentation pieces, or cheesy grocery store romance novels. However, now and then you may want to simulate the effect, either for a project that you will digitize or for a comp for a prospective job.

I embossed this design on the paper, and then rubbed a "Distress Ink" stamp pad (available at hobby stores) lightly over the raised areas to make them more visible. ~𝓡

As long as you've got the stencil tools out, try embossing into the thin sheets of metal you can get in the art and craft stores. I prefer the thinner cuts, the .003, 40 gauge. ~R

There are all kinds of embossing stencils in the craft stores. They are usually punched out of thin but rigid metal or heavy plastic and made to use with a lightbox and an embossing stylus. Unfortunately, most of these commercial templates tend to be cutesy themes (hearts, birdies, bunnies) and are totally dysfunctional for the serious designer.

A simple typeface stencil, or a square, circle, or oval might be useful, but most of the rest are best used for making your sister's handmade baby shower invitations.

Since I don't have the tools to make stencils out of metal, I use the blank stencil plastic available at the craft store. By tracing my letterforms or images on the material with a Sharpie and then cutting them out with a new X-acto blade, I can create very decent embossing stencils. I have also been known to use my large collection of inking templates leftover from the 1970s for embossing stencils—circles, ovals, squares, triangles, etc.

When I was in Egypt, I was captivated with the stencils that were painted on every home in the Nubian villages. So I got me a stencil cutting tool (shown on the next page) because I plan to put Nubian stencils all over my New Mexico home. This tool comes in very handy for cutting stencils to emboss graphic projects. See how everything works together? ~R

157

To make blind embossed images, it's handy to have a lightbox (portable ones can be quite inexpensive) and an embossing stylus.

1 Because the ink might crack on the edges of the area where you are going to hand emboss, I recommend you leave it clear of ink, as in the example above.

2 Cut a piece of stencil material large enough to fit the image or letterforms you want to emboss.

Carefully trace your image on the stencil material with a fine-tip felt pen. I use my lightbox for this process. If you don't have a lightbox, tape the image and the stencil sheet to a window and trace it.

3 With a sharp X-acto knife, on your cutting mat carefully cut out the image or text to make a stencil.

Remember, when making a stencil, any counters (the holes) in letters will fall right out unless you create little attachment pieces (as shown below). You can cut these pieces off at the very last moment, after you've got a good stencil rubbing around the counter.

This is an embossing tool. It comes in handy for all kinds of things.

When cutting out the stencil, cut thin attachment strips to hold the counters in place.

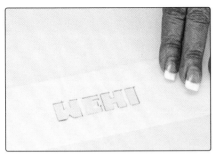

4 Turn your stencil over so it is wrong-reading (reversed), and place it on the lightbox.

5 Turn the paper on which you want to emboss face down; line it up perfectly with your embossing stencil.

If you want extra security (not a bad idea), you can fasten down your stencil and digital print with tape or drafting dots to make sure they don't move.

6 Using a medium-point stylus, rub very carefully but firmly on the back of the image, pushing the paper into the stencil.

You don't want to tear the paper or crack the ink, so use light but firm pressure. Go over the area several times to stretch the paper slowly and to smooth out the ridges left by the ball tip on the stylus.

Rub thoroughly so you don't get stylus marks. You must be careful—if you are too rough, you will tear the paper; if you are using photo paper, you might crack the surface of your digital print.

7 If you are careful, it is quite easy to create a great facsimile of what an embossing die would do.

If you discover that you love stencils and embossing, invest a few dollars in a handy little stencil cutter, shown below. It's much easier to melt through thick stencil film than to cut it with a knife.

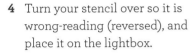

34 Gold-Stamp the Paper

Tools and materials

- Embossing stylus
- Paper project
- Lightbox, ideally
- Liquid Leaf paint
- Small brush suitable for oil paint
- Turpentine or turpenoid to clean the brush

Or use a metal leafing pen instead of painting with Liquid Leaf

You can create a gold-stamped effect on any project. This is great not only for comps and mockups, but for projects that you plan to digitize in which you want that gold-stamp look.

In this example, I'm embossing as in the previous chapter, and painting over that emboss, so the image is *raised*. You can also *de*boss a word or image and paint it gold, which makes it look like the gold leaf was stamped *into* the paper—just be sure that your stencil is right-reading instead of wrong-reading, and press into the *front* of the paper, not the back.

Keep in mind that shiny metals are hard to scan, so any project with metal or metal leaf might have to be photographed instead.

1 As in the previous chapter, create your stencil and get your project ready. This time I'm using a project where the text that I'm going to emboss is printed on the page. I'm going to paint over it anyway, and the inked text gives me a solid outline to stay within as I paint the gold leaf on.

2 Rub your image into the stencil, as explained on page 159.

3 Here you can see the raised, embossed text (MEHI).

4 Now paint those embossed letters with Liquid Leaf. You have to access your inner eye-surgeon craftsmanship and paint very carefully.

You can flick tiny little blips off with your X-acto knife, but you still need to be very tidy and exact if you want this to look good.

35 Metal-Leaf an Image

Tools and materials

- Substrate: canvas, watercolor paper, wood, Bristol board, metal, ceramic, glass, etc.
- Basecoat of acrylic paint (try red oxide, black, or yellow ocher)
- Metal leaf adhesive size
- Metal leaf (an alloy of inexpensive metals)
- Metal leaf sealer
- Small watercolor brush
- Large, soft watercolor brush

You can also use:
- Metallic graphic art tape
- Krylon Leafing Pens
- Opaque metallic pens
- Liquid Leaf product

After spending three weeks in Italy looking at all the religious paintings slathered in gold leaf, I went through my "gilt phase" where nearly everything I did had metal leaf on it. It's so easy to do and so fancy that it's hard not to gild everything in sight.

Real gold leaf is very expensive and comes in a little "book" at your art supply store. I have never bought *gold leaf* myself (except to decorate my truffles—yes, real gold leaf is edible). Instead, I use the *metal leaf* made out of inexpensive metals and tinted to look like gold, silver, copper, etc. This material does not have the brilliance or transparency that real gold leaf has (and is *not* edible!) but then I'm not usually creating Simone Martini's *Annunciation* for the Uffizi.

Using patina techniques (see Chapter 8), you can create an aged effect on metal leafing quite well. I particularly like to mix the brilliant metal against crusty aging affects.

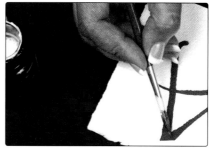

1   Trace or draw an image directly on your substrate—right reading.

    If you want your image to be raised off the page, create it with modeling paste (see Chapter 7). Round out the edges and corners with your brush. Let it dry.

2   Carefully paint the image with the acrylic paint; the color you choose will eventually show through the cracks that will appear. I'm using Old World Red Basecoat from the Old World Art metal leaf set.

    Let it dry thoroughly.

3   Carefully paint the image with the special adhesive size. I purposely leave little areas free of adhesive so the basecoat will show through.

    Let it dry until tacky—read the directions on the bottle of your adhesive size.

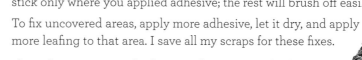

4   Gently pick up one of the ultra-thin leaves of metal leafing.

    Lay it carefully over the image.

5   Take your large, soft brush and tenderly brush the leafing off. It will stick only where you applied adhesive; the rest will brush off easily.

    To fix uncovered areas, apply more adhesive, let it dry, and apply more leafing to that area. I save all my scraps for these fixes.

6   If you don't want your leaf to tarnish, paint on a leafing sealer as a final step.

Leafing isn't very scan-friendly—it won't have the wonderful luminosity of the original piece.

36 Emboss with Powders

Tools and materials

- Image to emboss: digital print on matte paper
- Embossing fluid; glue pen or stamp pad
- Embossing powder
- Paint brush
- Heat gun

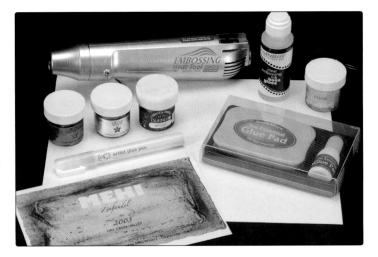

Embossing powders are fun little materials to play with. We have the scrapbookers to thank for its availability. There are many tasteful embossing powder colors to choose from—try gold, silver, white, or clear.

With the clear powder you can paint a color on your substrate, paint with the embossing fluid, sprinkle on the powder, heat it, and have a clear raised area just where you painted—a kind of spot varnish effect.

You will have to purchase a heat gun from a craft store to make this product work. A heat gun cannot be replaced with a hair dryer—the hair dryer does not get even close to hot enough.

Note! *You can't do this process on photo paper. The heat gun blisters the paper.*

Design your own stamps, then use an embossing fluid stamp pad to stamp your substrate, sprinkle on the powder of your choice, and heat.

Make an assembly line in your office to create personally embossed graphics for your own short run of promotional, greeting, or thank-you cards to your clients—stamp, powder, brush off, heat.

1 For this technique you need to get clear embossing fluid onto your image for the powder to stick to. You can stamp it (as I am doing here, with my own handmade stamp), or you can paint the fluid on to your piece with a brush.

The embossing fluid stays wet longer than regular stamping inks or paint, but make sure it is still wet when you shake on the embossing powder.

If you think it might be a bit too dry, give it a blow of huh-breath (the kind of breath you use to warm your hands, not to blow out candles).

2 Shake the embossing powder gently over the image on the board. The area where you painted the embossing fluid should be wet and the powder will stick there.

Or cut the end of a tiny straw at a 45-degree angle and use it as a mini scoop—scoop up a bit of powder and just put it on the area you need. This way you can use several different colors of powders on the same image.

—continued

Tip: *To prevent the embossing powder from sticking to the paper where you don't want it, invest a couple of dollars in an anti-static pad. Use it to wipe over your paper before you stamp or paint to prevent the powder from adhering to your page and getting melted on in places where you don't want it.*

 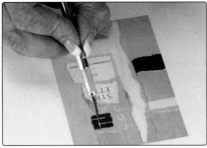 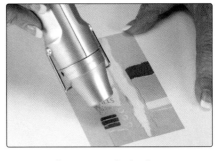

3 Pour the extra powder off your board back into the container, or at least onto a piece of paper so you can later pour it back into the container.

Flick off any grains of powder outside the image area.

4 Use an X-acto knife to delicately scrape off any little grains of powder that hang on in spite of your gentle flick.

5 Heat the area with the heat gun (a hair dryer won't work; it's not hot enough) until the embossing powder melts.

Be careful not to burn the powder by holding the gun too close! If you burn it, the powder will bubble and run, which doesn't look at all like that foil-stamp effect you're after.

(However, the melted powder certainly is "a look" and you might want to experiment with it. Melt a spoonful of the powder in a small metal container and pour it on in a random pattern. Take care to not burn yourself.)

Tip! *When heating the embossing powders, hold the paper up to eye level and watch as you heat. You'll see the powder change color and get shiny and then you'll know exactly when it's all done.*

~R

This CD cover incorporates gold-powder embossing on Lizzie's signature.

These gift cards have a human touch in the embossed images.

Combine Techniques!

Combine the riches—the pieces below include handmade paper, paper collage, metal collage, metal letterforms, splattered metal leafing pen, found objects, poured paint, a found piece of old rusting copper, metal leafing, and more. The trick is to keep your eyes open for possibilities and have drawers full of these items to work with. So go to your studio and get busy!

Illustrative Techniques

Even though I can draw a little, I never thought I could "illustrate." Why, I didn't have thirty units of upper division credits in illustration, so of course I couldn't be an "illustrator."

However, a cocky young student of mine looked at me in wonder when I asked if he had considered being an illustrator *and* a designer. "But, I *am* an illustrator," he exclaimed. Well, if he could be an illustrator with only a community college vocational degree, then just maybe I was buying into the elitism that labels talent by education and background rather than by actual output. I decided then and there that I, myself, could "illustrate." That night I got out my polymer clay tools and got busy.

Don't let your preconceived notions limit you. You can't draw? That doesn't mean you can't illustrate just beautifully. Try using some of the wonderful techniques offered here, and you just might surprise yourself. I did.

Illustrative Techniques

There are many ways to illustrate a design piece besides drawing.

37 Scratchboard

With scratchboard you can create imagery that has a distinctive human touch. Even if you're not an illustrator, this technique can bring out interesting shapes and textures useful for many projects.

See pages 172–177.

38 Found-Object Art

For your next project, consider building an illustrative piece using objects found in your home, studio, garage, junk yard, neighborhood park, or craft store.

See pages 178–185.

39 Polymer Clay

Polymer clay is irresistibly enjoyable to work with. Let your inner kid take over and illustrate your next project with clay.

See pages 186–195.

40 Illustrate with Collage

Don't neglect the art of collage as a possibility for illustrative ideas. Collage lends itself to simple, suggestive imagery.

See pages 196–197.

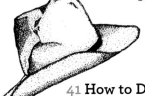

41 How to Draw if you Can't Draw

To those of us who are not illustrators, many projects are daunting or too expensive to produce. But here are a few techniques you can use to create some interesting illustrations all by yourself.

See pages 198–203.

The laptop is off the table. Let's get out the art supplies!

Join Carmen in the studio for a day of texture-making and handmade illustration techniques. Get your hands dirty with paint and glue and paper and knives and hammers and brushes.

Let Carmen show you how to take advantage of simple materials and low-tech equipment to make your own sophisticated and unique images to use in your professional work.

Sunday . September 9
10 A.M. to 3:30 P.M.
Lunch provided
Materials supplied
$85 per person

To reserve your spot,
call 707.555.1202

1033 Volumnia Drive
Windsor . California

I built the little set pictured in the poster with my beloved father's help, and then I proceeded to collect and create all the miniature art supplies and furniture.

I love black and white, so of course I had to use that as a motif in my little dream studio.

As you can see, I created a clay sculpture of myself, and a wonderful student of mine, Ganeen Vega, sewed the little clothes for me — a seamstress I am not!

As you can tell, we are about to do some wonderful technique at my upcoming workshop, and I am putting my paper in the tray, ready to use, with my tiny little sea sponge.

171

37 Scratch into Scratchboard

Tools and materials

- Essdee Scraper Board, or other clayboard or scratchboard
- Sume-i ink or India ink
- Fine-tip ballpoint pen or stylus
- Water media brushes, broad and fine-point
- Scratch tools: Either a set you can buy from an art store, or use a straight pin, a nail, your X-acto knife, or any scraping tool
- Graphite paper (optional, shown on opposite page)

Scratchboard is one of my favorite materials. There's something about that scratched line that really says "human touch." To me it harkens back to our ancestors, to those extraordinary stylized images scraped onto the walls of caves and canyon rocks, images that inspire my imagination.

Scratchboard is the designer's friend because it's easy to use, scans well, and is perfect for logos, spot illustrations, and other custom graphic treatments.

The only way to get superior results with this medium is to use the best materials. The cheap, flimsy, waxy stuff should be left in the store. I like Essdee Scraper Board from England—it has a beautiful clay coating and scrapes "like buttah, lovey."

You're going to trace or draw your image onto the board,
ink right over it, then scratch into the ink to create the illustration.

1 First, draw your image on tracing paper (or draw directly on the board, hard enough to make an indent, and skip to Step 4).

2 Trace the design with a fine-tip ballpoint pen or a stylus onto the scratchboard using graphite paper (see page 21).

3 Press fairly hard so you get a slight indentation into the scratchboard.

—continued

Tip! *To get your image from your computer or copier onto tracing paper, tape a smaller piece of tracing paper along its top edge and corners to a piece of regular bond paper. Then send that through your copy machine or printer. Make sure the taped end heads in first.* ~ℛ

You can get such amazingly fine detail in scratchboard that sometimes it's useful to work through a magnifying loupe or a desk magnifier.

4 On the scratchboard, carefully paint the areas that you plan to scratch into with an opaque ink such as sume-i or India ink.

Use a good water media brush with a nice point, but don't use the same brushes you use with watercolors because it's hard to get the ink completely out of the bristles—the leftover black ink will later muddy up your transparent colors.

Don't worry about painting around fine details—the indentations you traced will show through the ink.

Tip! *You don't want reflections when you scan the image, so be careful of the ink you choose. Some inks, such as certain India inks, contain shellac and can dry with shiny spots that reflect in the scanner. Of course, you can always do a little fixing in Photoshop, but I hate spending time fixing.* ~C

5 Let the inked surface dry thoroughly. Scratchboard has a clay surface coating and if you scratch into the material while it is still damp, it's like playing in the mud and you won't get a crisp, clean line. Use your hair dryer or heat gun if you're in a big hurry.

Once the piece is totally dry, you'll see your detail indentations showing through the inked image.

Alternatively, you can always ink the entire board or buy a pre-inked board and trace your image on top of the ink.

6 Use your scratch tools to scratch into your image with solid little flicking strokes. The whole reason to use this technique is to get those splendid scratchy lines, so let them show—don't clean it up too much. If you don't have scratch tools, use a straight pin or needle—stick it in the eraser end of a pencil. Or use your X-acto knife.

Use a tissue or brush to wipe off the ink dust you create; don't blow it off or it gets up in your sinuses and all over your table!

7 If you get scratch-happy and accidentally remove spots of ink that you need, just re-ink the area and scratch back into it when it's dry. As long as you haven't scratched all the way down to the chipboard, you can work and re-work the illustration until you're satisfied with the results.

8 Once your piece is almost finished, look it over in the light. If there are small areas that need touch-ups, use a fine-tip black felt pen.

In this example, I experimented with Dr. Ph. Martin's brown (instead of black) India ink. As you can see, it was impossible to get good, solid coverage because it's not completely opaque ink. It makes an interesting effect, but it's more difficult to scratch through the many layers of ink. ~R

On the left (above) is the sort of drawing you might automatically create, scratching white lines where you would typically draw black lines. It creates the effect of drawing on a chalkboard with chalk. This isn't really what you want.

On the right, you can see that the black lines were created by scratching out *around* those lines. It's more work, but the end result is much more interesting and looks less like a negative.

A project using scratchboard

Here is an example of putting together a short-run promotional piece using a variety of handmade techniques. The project is for our graphic design internship program at Santa Rosa Junior College in northern California.

I bought some beautiful handmade paper and had the campus print shop cut the sheets down the middle and in 4½" x 13" strips, saving the deckle (the rough edges of the handmade paper) on the ends. We used these for the covers.

Darrell Perry, my design partner on this project, wrote the little story about an intern who helps a design firm grow to be strong and successful. He illustrated it using scratchboard. Darrell also created the initial caps in scratchboard, designed a sticker, and created a vellum band with the return address.

We found a paper preprinted with a marbled texture we liked. For an extra touch of class, we created a vellum overleaf (shown above, first page).

The printing department at the college printed 150 copies and trimmed them up for us.

There were two successful graphic design firms right next door to each other. Both were very popular and received business from local and surrounding merchants of the Santa Rosa area.

One day an Applied Graphics student named Johnny from the Santa Rosa Junior College was out looking for a position as an intern. He came upon the first design firm and decided to inquire about a position. Johnny spoke with the owner but was turned away. As he walked out onto the sidewalk, Johnny noticed the second design firm and thought he would give it a try.

I got out my trusty sewing machine and stitched all the little booklets together with an earthy, ocher-colored thread.

Because we didn't have enough money in the budget for a die for our stickers, we printed them off on Avery round stickers on my laser printer and trimmed them with our X-acto knives.

Well, some people knit;
I cut things out
with my X-acto knife.
~C

Johnny walked next door into the second design firm and once more inquired about an intern position, but this time he was hired.

The second design firm was very happy with Johnny's work; he became a valuable asset and helped them get a lot of work done. The first design firm started to lose business as the second firm continued to grow and grow. Eventually, the first design firm couldn't keep up. The owner was forced to stop doing business as a designer and open a hot dog stand.

O.K. so have one on us—a hot dog, that is, at your favorite place and let us talk to you about our very successful internship program. Just fill out the little card and we'll contact you by phone. You never know, life could be very good.

For more information don't hesitate to call either Bev Smith, Internship Coordinator, at 707.527.4604 or Carmen Karr, Applied Graphics Program Coordinator, at 707.527.4909.

The cover wraps around from the back to overlap the front
and is held together with a printed vellum band and the sticker.

38 Illustrate with Found-Object Art

Tools and materials

- Canvases
- Glass
- Various miniature items
- Hot glue gun
- Graphic art tapes
- Hobby miter saw
- Miniature molding
- Miniature architectural elements
- Brush
- X-acto knife with new blade
- Sheetrock knife
- Cutting mat
- Hammer
- Painter's masking tape
- Spray paints
- Metal leafing supplies
- E-6000 adhesive
- Lots of found stuff

Found-object illustration (or *assemblage,* as it is known in the fine arts realm) is a very popular technique for creating unique and eye-catching visuals. This is a fairly modern process, and for the graphic designer it can be quite a useful method for creating one-of-a-kind images to use in appropriate projects.

The supplies listed to the left and shown above are what I used for the particular example in this chapter. Every found-object piece of art will use different tools and objects that you'll discover along the way. But don't be limited by just what you have on hand—consider how the possibilities will expand if you invest in a few nifty tools!

Designer's skills

To create effective found-object illustration, a designer must use a variety of skills.

- It's good to have an eye for the possibilities of found objects and how they could be used to communicate in another context.

- Being an organized pack rat and somewhat of a shopper is also important because you need bits and pieces to work with.

- Some hand-building skills are useful because for this type of illustration you might need to cut, saw, hammer, drill, sand, paint, glue, sew, model clay, etc.

- Finally, the designer should have a professional way to image the illustration. There are ways to scan found-object illustrations; however, for commercial publication most illustrations will need to be photographed with professional lighting and a high-quality digital camera.

Resources for found objects

One of the best places to start looking for interesting found objects is in your own **home and garage.** Old pieces of home improvement projects, scraps of wood, hardware, nuts, bolts, wire, leftover metal—all provide great fodder for the found-object illustrator. Your junk drawer can yield aging office supplies, a lonely earring, an interesting key, some cool buttons . . . I'm sure you get the picture.

The designer can also **shop** flea markets, thrift stores, recycling centers, garage sales, antique shops, and junkyards for interesting stuff. And don't forget when you **stroll** along railroad tracks to look for castoff iron pieces.

Your local **hardware store** provides a wide variety of interesting metal pieces, pipes, wires, plugs, nuts, bolts, screen, tile, etc. Also, this is where you can stock up on industrial-strength adhesives, fasteners, and specialized painting supplies. The sales staff can help you choose the right products for the materials you have decided to use.

Ask lots of questions because you are often using materials unfamiliar to the artist and, believe me, getting everything to stick together can be a bit of an issue when you have metal, wood, glass, plastic, and paper all on the same illustration.

Of course, **craft and hobby stores** have lots of doodads, beads, papers, miniature things, little doll things, etc. Just remember that many of these items can be a little on the cutesy side for a serious illustrator. Nonetheless, that tiny Uncle Sam suit that would be just perfect for your presidential parody will be there and at such an excellent price.

Nature is also a perfect resource for found objects. Sticks, dried moss, grasses, flowers, leaves, stones, shells, feathers—wow, your imagination will go wild once it's tuned in to the found-art possibilities.

Not all your found-object illustrations need to last forever and ever. You can easily make **perishable illustrations** with fruits, vegetables, candy, cakes, and fresh flowers. Of course, you would need to have your camera set up and ready to go if you choose to go with a perishable arrangement. You don't want a wilting illustration.

Organization for found-object illustrators

I am often asked how I keep all my "stuff" organized because students wonder how they have room for all these bits and pieces and, more importantly, how to find them once they do collect them.

Well, the key is moderation and organization. You don't need to have *everything* on hand at all times. You just need to know where to find your pickings when you need them. Learn to be a great scout!

So while some acquisitiveness is useful (you know, free stuff or those one-of-a-kind sale items), it's important to stay on good terms with your family, roommates, and neighbors by being realistic about your storage options.

I use inexpensive, transparent plastic bins to store my collectibles. I find that if I label my bins very elegantly, my husband is less likely to get on my case about all the "junk" I'm collecting. Besides, even though my bins are see-through, some fine but unlabeled goods can look suspiciously like other very fine unlabeled goods and I don't want to spend hours looking though my boxes for that motherboard from my old PowerMac that I need for a great illustration I have in mind.

Obviously, every found-object illustration has different criteria and steps to create it. However, by going step-by-step through one of my illustration projects, I am sure you can get a great idea of how to use a variety of tools and materials to make your own found-object art.

~C

Creating a triptych of found art

In the following example I'm making an illustration to go along with a magazine article about taking a mental vacation from your office to beat stress and revive your soul. I decided to do a triptych (set of three) showing office windows and a chair chained to the floor, but the chair escapes.

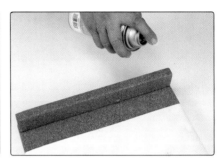

1   I bought three primed (pre-coated with gesso) canvases, each 10" x 12" x 2".

   I taped off the bottom of two of the canvases with painter's tape, then painted the top portions with copper metallic acrylic paint.

2   I wanted to create windows with blue skies, so when the copper paint was dry, I taped window shapes with painter's masking tape. In those two spaces I painted blue skies with fluffy clouds.

   The third canvas was totally sky. I set that aside to use later.

3   After my blue sky rectangles had dried, I masked off the top of my illustrations with white butcher paper. I found two pieces of wood and glued them on the canvases with my hot glue gun to make identical ledges. I then sprayed these ledges and the bottom portions of my illustrations with Speckle Stone spray paint (you could also use Krylon Make It Stone! spray paint).

4   I had two pieces of glass that fit my window rectangles (your local glass shop can provide you with glass cut to your specifications). I wanted one of my windows to look like it had been broken, so I wrapped it in a piece of craft felt.

5   I used a punch and hammer to give the felt/glass sandwich a solid whack. The glass broke perfectly.

—continued

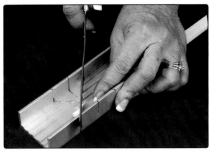

6 I then cut small moldings with my hobby miter saw to make frames for the windows.

7 I painted my moldings and two small lintels (horizontal supports across the tops of windows or doors) that I had bought at a dollhouse supply store with the same Speckle Stone spray paint I used to paint the ledges.

8 I put the glass and molding in place and glued them on both canvases with Amazing Goop, an adhesive that glues just about anything to anything. You can find it in a hardware store.

9 I glued on the lintels to finish the windows.

10 I wanted wings on the office chairs, so I bought white feathers at the crafts store. I cut them to fit the miniature office chairs that I had purchased at the dollhouse supply store.

11 I glued my little office chairs in place.

12 I wanted straps to convey the sense of feeling trapped and then breaking out, so I used thin wires and connectors I found in a discarded blueprint machine at school. To create tiny plugs, I nipped off the tops of sewing pins and forced them into my ledges with pliers.

13 I glued the connectors to the wires and then put a bit of glue on the ends before I "plugged" them in to the eensy pins.

14 Now to finish that third canvas: I wanted the last miniature chair to really soar, so I made another pair of wings, more abundant than the first set.

15 I carefully glued my wings on to the chair.

16 Then I glued my last little office chair soaring in the clear, blue sky on my third painted canvas.

—continued

When it came time to use the triptych in the magazine spread, it seemed more appropriate to have the third piece simply show the missing chair, as if it had escaped, and use the full blue canvas of the chair soaring through the sky on the second page of the spread.

mental health essay

Heresy borsch-boil starry a board borsch boil gam plate lung, lung a gore inner ladle wan hearse torn coiled Mutterfill.

Mutterfill worsen mush offer torn, butted hatter putty gut borsch-boil tame, an off oiler pliers honor taTne, door moist cerebrated worse Casing. Casing worsted sickened basement, any hatter betting orphanage off .526 (punt fife toe sex).

Casing worse gut lurking, an furry poplar, spatially wetter putty gull coiled Anybally. Anybally worse Casing's sweat-hard, any harpy cobble wandered toe gat merit, bought Casing worse toe pore toe becalm Anybally's horsebarn (boil pliers honor Mutterfill tame dint gat mush offer celery; infect, day gut nosing atoll).

Bought less gat earn wetter starry.

Wan dare, inner Mutterfill borsch boil pork, door scar stud lack disk inner lest in-ink. Water disgorging saturation! Oiler Mutterfill rotors, setting inner grinstance, war failing furry darn inner mouse.

ESCAPE
without leaving your
OFFICE

We know you're stuck at your desk, but try these five mental escapades to relieve the stress and maintain your health.

BY SCARLETT FLORENCE

Bought, watcher thank chewed hopping den. Soddenly wan offer Mutterfill pliers hitter shingle, an in udder plier gutter gnats toe beggar. Soda war ptomaine earn basis. Bust off oil, Casing hamshelf, Mutterfill's cerebrated better, worse combing ope toe bet.

Whinny met kraut inner in stance sore Casing combing, day stuttered toe clabber hens an yowl, "Date's casing Attar bore, Casing." An whinny hansom sickened base ment sundered confidentially ope tutor plat, oiler Mutterfill rotors shorted.

Putty ladle Anybally, setting oil buyer shelf inner grinstance, worse furry prod offer gat lurking loafer. Lack oiler udder pimple, Anybally worse shore debt oilboy Casing worse garner winner boil gam fur Mutterfill. Soddenly wan offer Mutterfill

53

1. CLOSE
your eyes and . . .

Meresy borsch-boil starry a board borsch boil gam plate lung, lung a gore inner ladle wan hearse torn coiled Mutterfill.

Mutterfill worsen mush offer torn, butted hatter putty gut borsch-boil tame, an off oiler pliers honor taTne, door moist cerebrated worse Casing. Casing worsted sickened basement, any hatter betting orphanage off .526 (punt fife toe sex).

Casing worse gut lurking, an furry poplar, spatially wetter putty gull coiled Anybally. Anybally worse Casing's sweat-hard, any harpy cobble wandered toe gat merit, bought Casing worse toe pore toe becalm Anybally's horsebarn (boil pliers honor Mutterfill tame dint gat mush offer celery; infect, day gut nosing atoll).

Bought less gat earn wetter starry. Wan dare, inner Mutterfill borsch boil pork, door scar stud lack disk inner lest in-ink. Water disgorging saturation! Oiler Mutterfill rotors, setting inner grinstance, war failing furry darn inner mouse.

Audrey HEPBURN

Wem voloria dolup tatquia voluptur anno nestium adit mint fugia natum voluptas in nosapidis asit aut dollia adit aut il ipidior iatemol uptur. Cid eat hilal ipsundi caboresequam fugiam et lit apis pla quiate velest lient reium quas sitam inullupis te molupta susda nisque nusda serchitia vollacc abore, nonqu ossitat dolupta ersped unt dolor accabo. Ita quia saes verspid magnihil ex et, in rate vere vele nimilitin rehenim porectat.

Ta pe ra vellabori imporrovit magnatur. Ellorision non nim repuda doluptiam, qui consecus.

dolupturest, sinveli simi llore nulparc iendem expelique ne ditatia is id quate nonse con et eos eum dolorempor ab mus pores nosape conse ction pedipidem rept.

Et volorec atiae. Rect. Timo ommolupit incnt aruptam eaquodiorum facea quae eum, susandant facearum ipidenihita este omnis denis et dolor as sitatur, consequati que nis quibus etur serumqui odiae nus.

Omnit, ut faces ratus, quia quiaepe prent, omnim qui ute omnit mostemposam litatur acim dolecto tatur. Uptatur

"One thing that struck me about her, apart from her charm and elegance, was her ability to make herself loved and admired by women as well as men."

Hubert de Givenchy

Oluptat unti doluptatur nero omnimin non pore, imet et optatur eperibusam reptio excest aria etus as aditior erchill endelesedis dionsedi corepercis adis quam, similig endanis quatur. Et ipsus aut aut quisse- quunt alit et magnis molupti busandae ni te inullaut lam re, qui volorias verovitianis quo invel excerferum rerum inverum ut eatum rae exerspernati corent ut ex eturibus eostioribus.

Rest, as aut la sit auditiatem ate pa prem as modisitae quia, quas inctium re, sit, nimodi te con remolor itiuritiassi qui rent essenis nis earcilitat at vendis- trum re pa verum eum vel eum aliqui utet, apelent enitia eos arumquiat apienet odi ipit re vidus iminctat.

Gitissi nverehe ndaecatus estiust omnihici ut quodi test occus, sintore conserum sum solorporae pore voloreped qua

urne pore voluptas undam, ipis voluptus arisimaio berem ation pa doluptae. Aximoluptae eos nobis ex et rectem. Et aut qui sin parum ipicim recum quas sae sit apitios ipienis sitius nemolecaecte vera quam aute volupti isquam, consequi opta volorpore, sim ad mi, officia poris et quid qui a porpor aut is magnam laccum, occus arum faccus volest parum, simo dolestianda aliant que porit aceaquas cosam expedis molpta quiatem eatem arciend ipsant.

Sedia iusti cum et omnim essitionsed quaeculpa de sap volupicia poreiuremos enim autemporae cum quidunti corem aut enimossin consed exceprem volorru ptasimp orempores is rest, essi ut que ventotate perciet prati nesci- tatem estium acero dolorrum repere consequasit a dolup- tae porempera nim a con pro

blati dolupta ducita cum rem volores dolorem volendeles aut ea aborio il inctur rentio quas seriam eatur ressuntiste estrum inctios volor alit, vellectem. Et labo. Picilitatium sum latur a sandi unt et pero blam. Ari ommolo qui te ex et eos utcat hicium veliqui consequiam velia doloriaes apiet dolo tem aut plic totat ad quibus eturissequi cus imint doluptatio denisciist que vent vidit porepta nus nisin est

preperumqui ut odistibus rem quibusapide exero voluptae. Tatia num eum autecto officie nectes accupti aut fuga. Ut aut hilis remque voluptatam re, ut dolupid quatem fuga. Igender feriamus enditiur, sunda nula inctatque lita dolendita ven dandi quiam seceperrore.

— Ucimi Operrami

This piece, designed by Gaia Sikora, is illustrated with found objects that express the essence of Audrey Hepburn.

A rusted steel beam in the desert—with some vinyl lettering applied—becomes a focal point for a poster.

A TASTE OF SHAKESPEARE

Taste the wines, ales, and spirits mentioned in the **SHAKESPEAREAN** plays— malmsey, canary, rhenish, bastard, mead, sack, possets, and more!

Hosted at The Mermaid Tavern in Santa Fe, New Mexico

SUNDAY APRIL 1 5–7 P.M.

Benefit Tickets $45
Tickets must be reserved in advance
must be 21 years of age
sponsored by the Mary Sidney Society

Mermaid Tavern
What things we have seen done at the Mermaid!

39 Illustrate with Clay

Tools and materials

Required:

- Polymer clay: Sculpey, Fimo, Premo! (or other brands)
- Baking pan, plus baking parchment paper or tin foil

Used in this project:

- Armature wire, jewelry wire
- Tin foil
- Smooth piece of glass, plexi-glass, marble, or ceramic tile on which to roll out clay
- Clay roller (not shown)
- Hand-crank pasta maker
- Garlic press or clay extruder
- Cutters (clay blade, craft scissors, pieces of pens, cake decorating tips)
- Tools such as knitting needles, dental tools, clay tools, manicure set, scoring stylus, clay shapers, pliers
- Gauze tape
- Metal stamps
- E-6000 adhesive

Clay sculpture is easy to set up and clean up. It can be whimsical, exaggerated, stylized, colorful, and just plain fun. However, it can also be a great tool for illustration because it provides images with engaging dimensionality.

Don't let the list of tools or the photo scare you—these are just what I used for the sample in this chapter. You can create wonderful objects with almost no tools at all.

Once polymer clay is baked, you can paint it, drill it, sand it, glue it, add other clay pieces and rebake, and more. It's amazing.

Polymer clay is a wonderful product. It doesn't dry out in the air so it doesn't need to be babied like the Play-Doh we used as kids. However, polymer clay is much easier to shape if it is body temperature and "conditioned."

The easiest way to condition your clay is with a pasta maker. You can do this without a pasta maker, but the little machine is so efficient. I bought several manual pasta makers at the local flea market for $5 each (I guess a lot of people have good intentions of making their own pasta and find it's too much trouble).

Amaco and Makin's both make a "pasta machine" specifically for clay for about $25. You can find them online or in most hobby/craft stores.

Do NOT use the kind of pasta machine that also mixes the dough, and do NOT use the pasta machine for food after you've put clay through it!

I use Sculpey as my polymer clay of choice. It is strong, available, I can find large pieces of it, and it's easy to use. Nonetheless, it is certainly not the only product out there.

Premo! Sculpey is another clay from Sculpey that is a little more difficult to condition but creates a stronger final product. Fimo Soft and Fimo Classic are similar in that Fimo Soft is easier to condition and work with than Fimo Classic (although both are more difficult than Sculpey). And there are polymer clays made specifically for fine details, for puppet faces, for lightweight jewelry making, etc.!

I realize you probably won't be creating a mermaid exactly like the one in this next example, but if you follow along, you'll learn a lot of little tricks about working with polymer clay that you can apply to your own project. ~C

I wanted to make a special illustration for Robin's Mermaid Tavern in Santa Fe where she holds Shakespeare readings with her enthusiastic pals. I wanted it to be three dimensional so I used one of my favorite mediums—clay sculpture.

~ C

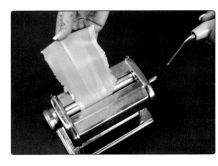

1   Before you make a sculpture, you *must* condition the clay: Slice off a thick piece and use a roller to flatten it by hand to about ⅜". Then roll it through a manual pasta maker about fifteen or twenty times (or squeeze and knead the clay until it is soft and pliable, if you don't have a pasta maker).

2   If you want to **make a special color,** take two or three other clay colors and mix them by rolling them together several times through the pasta maker (or in your hands). Here I combined yellow and bright green clay to make a light sea-foam–green color.

3   Because polymer clay will crack when baked if it's too thick (plus it's expensive), it's best to make an aluminum foil framework, or armature, for large pieces.

To prevent the foil from showing lumps in your finished outer layer, first wrap a thin layer of any color clay around the foil. Just roll out some clay, wrap it around the foil base, and start molding your shape. You'll probably need more than one thin layer before you apply your final colored one.

I'm not wrapping around the back of my piece since this figure will be affixed to a sign board. However, if you want to photograph your sculpture from all sides, finish the back as well.

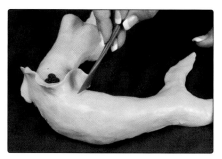

4   Put your final layer on top of the protective layer. Here I've added the mermaid torso onto the fish tail.

5   I wanted to give the mermaid's tail some fish-scale texture so I wrapped the clay with my fishnet stockings and pressed the pattern into the clay.

You can use all sorts of things to press patterns into your clay—rubber stamps, forks, coins, pens and pencils, paper clips, tenderizer tools, textured wallpaper, leaves and bark, your own custom stamps (see Chapter 43), etc.

6   To create the head, cover a small ball of aluminum foil with flesh-colored clay—roll them together in your hands. This ball should be covered with considerably more clay than the torso or tail because you want to carve features into it and you don't want to hit the foil when you do so. I would say add a half inch of clay at the least.

7   Using whatever tools you like, start forming the nose, cheeks, eye sockets, and chin. Here I'm using a favorite tool—my knitting needle—to form the features.

8   To make hair for the figure, try using a garlic press. I have several different garlic presses so I can have different thicknesses of strands, depending on the look I want for a 'do.

You can also buy an inexpensive clay extruder that pushes clay through various holes to create hair, thin ropes of clay, or other shapes, as shown on page 194.

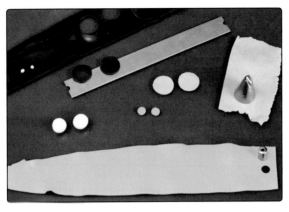

9 Take your time to carefully put the eyes together:

- First roll two identical little balls of white clay for the eyeballs.
- Make two *very tiny* white balls for the pupil highlights.
- Roll out a piece of black clay on the thinnest setting of your pasta maker (almost paper thin). Cut two circles of black clay using the back of a cake decorator tip or similar-sized cutter.
- Do the same with a piece of flesh-colored clay.
- For the irises, use something like the top of your mechanical pencil to punch out two little circles of clay in the eye color.

If your circles stick to the table surface, use your clay blade (see page 194) or X-acto knife to carefully lift them off.

10 To assemble the eyes, put a colored iris in the center of a white eyeball.

11 Affix the black pupil, making sure some of the iris can be seen.

12 Wrap the top of the eyeball with a larger circle of black clay—this gives the eye a shadow.

13 Put the flesh-colored clay over the black for the eyelid. Smooth it down carefully.

14 Put the tiny highlight dot where you want the eye to be directed. Repeat for the other eye. If the eyeballs are not identical, your creature will have a goofy look!

Remember, polymers are adhesives. When you put two pieces of clay together, they will glue to themselves as they bake. Do not add glue before baking!

~R

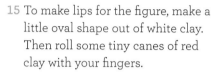

15 To make lips for the figure, make a little oval shape out of white clay. Then roll some tiny canes of red clay with your fingers.

If you have a clay extruder, you can use that to make canes.

16 Shape the canes around the white oval and mold the mouth carefully. A knitting needle makes a good tool to smooth the corners of the lips, or use one of your clay tools or any other smooth-tipped tool you have around the house/studio.

17 Very gently press the eyes, mouth, and hair to the head. You may have to carve off the backs of the eyeballs with your clay blade or a knife to make them fit in the eye sockets properly.

If you plan to add earrings, pierce the ears with a sharp tool.

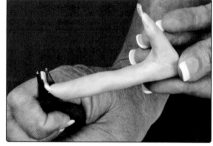

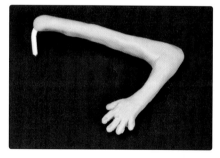

18 To give appendages some strength, use armature wire. Cut the length you need, leaving enough on the end to bend and affix to the clay torso. Armature wire bends very easily with pliers.

19 Bend the arm wire to make an elbow, then roll some flesh-colored clay around the wire. Create a bend in the wire at the shoulder to affix the arm.

20 To create the hands, add a piece of clay at the end and cut fingers with a clay blade or knife. Shape the fingers with a knitting needle or similar tool. Smooth the clay carefully.

21 Press details such as fingernails into the clay with something like a manicure tool.

22 Put the arms on the torso and smooth everything in place. You can affix items to your piece before you bake it as long as the items won't be melted by heat. I used shells to make a bathing suit top.

Place a piece of baking parchment or foil on a baking sheet. Place the head in a little nest of foil to keep it from rolling. Give it a good look before you bake. Hmmmm . . . I'm not so sure I have as much texture on that tail as I would like. What to do? I need to experiment.

23 After trying several things, I decided to use one of my little circle cutters. I cut all over the tail in an overlapping pattern and lifted the scales up a tad. Much better texture.

And now to bake. Sculpey bakes for 15 minutes at 275° (check the directions for your clay). Let cool.

24 Now for the fun part—embellishing!

- I gave our Mermaid a crown made from an old earring.
- I gave her a necklace.
- I made an armband from clay cut with decorative scissors and decorated with silver findings.
- I made tiny earrings from little shells and beads.
- Our Mermaid is, of course, reading one of Robin's favorite Shakespeare plays made from a little book and covered with a book jacket I created in InDesign.

- I found an appropriate typeface (Blackmoor), formatted "The Mermaid Tavern" in Illustrator, and printed it out. I transferred that lettering to my stained sign board with transfer paper.
- I metal-leafed the lettering, making sure to use a red base coat for that rough-edged, antique feeling (see Chapter 35).
- And then I glued our Mermaid and a pretty scallop shell in place using E-6000 glue.

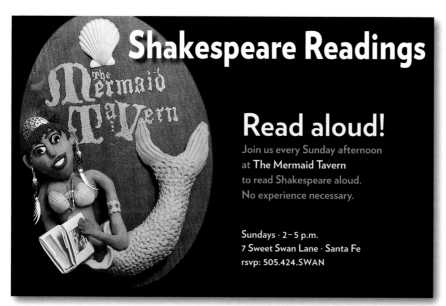

Shakespeare Readings

Read aloud!

Join us every Sunday afternoon at **The Mermaid Tavern** to read Shakespeare aloud. No experience necessary.

Sundays · 2 – 5 p.m.
7 Sweet Swan Lane · Santa Fe
rsvp: 505.424.SWAN

You can see how much impact a three-dimensional piece can add as an illustration.

The original now hangs proudly in the foyer of The Mermaid Tavern in Santa Fe.

Although it looks complex, the mermaid only took about three hours to create.

~C

I am fascinated with claymation and clay sculpture. Maybe it's because I have always liked models and dioramas. There was a time when I thought that the perfect use of my artistic skills would be to work for a museum as the graphic designer and model builder. But life took other paths and I never had the opportunity to pursue that dream.

I was enchanted by "The California Raisins" commercials from Will Vinton's studio and after that I searched for examples of clay sculpture and claymation illustrations wherever I could. One of my favorite contemporary illustrators is Chris Sickels who owns Red Nose Studio. His marvelous and charming characters illustrate everything from career development on the cover of *How* magazine to affordable health care in *AARP*. I was like a giddy groupie when I got a chance to talk to this unassuming young man at the *How Design Conference* in Chicago. He generously shared his techniques with me and answered my questions about clay sculpture. He showed me his little figures and even gave me a treasured copy of "The Red Thread Project" that he illustrated with clay.

This year I am finishing my own children's book—totally illustrated with clay sculpture figures and my own model building. So you see, life has a way of giving us chances to pursue our dreams one way or another. I may not be creating scenes of Navajo villages for the Natural History Museum, but I *am* getting to create something that is my own vision.   ~C

Experiment with polymer clay!

With polymer clay, you have many other options besides creating sculpture as a design element: texture a thin slab of clay as a background, press leaves into clay, emboss small clay tiles with letter stamps for a type headline, hand-cut tiles from clay and decorate them with paint to create a mosaic illustration. Once you've got some clay in your studio, you'll find ways to use it in your digital design, we guarantee.

Create letterforms

Either carve or build letterforms from this great polymer material. Or get one of the many lettering molds, as shown below.

Remember, you're a digital designer so you're not stuck with using the size of letters that come right out of the mold. Create them, bake them, paint them if you like, then scan your words and use them in your digital piece.

Extrude stuff

You can have terrific fun with an extruder, as shown below. It comes with a variety of tips so you can squeeze out hair or long ropes of shapes. Use the clay blade to slice tiny pieces of the extruded rope to use as decorative elements.

Tip! *A clay blade is indispensable. For example, use it to slice off excess clay from a mold, as shown here.*

Get to work!

You can create a great many simple illustrations with polymer clay and some kitchen tools (you don't even need to have a pasta maker). Do you have to design a postcard reminder for the dentist, the car lube place, the veterinarian? Make a little clay sculpture! Do you have a brochure to create for the local symphony, your favorite restaurant, the computer clinic, a moving company? Surely you can build a moving van out of clay! Expand your design horizons and consider clay as an illustrative medium. And as this example shows, you can combine the sculpture with one of your lovely textured backgrounds.

John Tollett built this puppy for the poster and used a splattered background (see Chapter 21) for a light-hearted, energetic look.

I grabbed some leaves from a flower bed, rolled polymer clay over them to get the veining, cut them out, shaped them as you see here, baked them, painted them with violet acrylic, then rubbed iridescent pastels into the texture to make it pop out. I affixed the leaves to a textured and painted background (see Chapter 7) I had created earlier.

195

40 Illustrate with Collage

Tools and materials

- Substrate to glue onto
- Papers to cut up
- Adhesives
- Scissors and/or X-acto knife
- Burnisher of some kind

HappyTree Farms **Guide**

This short chapter is a reminder that you can also use collage as an illustrative tool, not just for abstract backgrounds. In Chapters 29 and 30, Carmen explained in detail how to develop and assemble a collage. Here are a few samples of how simple shapes can be used to embellish certain graphic design and web projects, especially for those of us who can't draw.

Also experiment with combining collage with found objects (Chapter 38) to create three-dimensional illustrations. Oh, the possibilities! ~ℛ

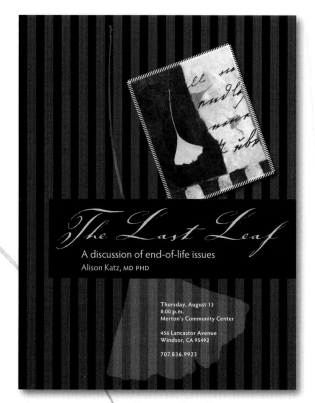

The little collage
*piece includes
a portion of a
background that
was sponged
and stamped.*

Council on
Domestic American Relationships

*Is the answer to
rising divorce rates
to make divorce more
difficult to obtain,
or to make it more
difficult to get married
in the first place?*

The Last Leaf

A discussion of end-of-life issues

Alison Katz, MD PHD

Thursday, August 13
8:00 p.m.
Merton's Community Center

456 Lancastor Avenue
Windsor, CA 95492

707.836.9923

*This poster uses a small piece of a collage as an
illustrative element. The large ginko leaf was scanned
and applied as a collage element directly in InDesign.*

Evanescent Wan Think, Itching Udder

Wan moaning, servile moor wicks letter, Violate worse inner fodder's vestibule guarding darn honor hens an niece, pecking bogs an warms offer vestibules. Soddenly shay nudist annulled badger-lore, home pimple cold "Carnal" Gatretch, combing entity guarding.

Gatretch worsen rallier carnal, hay worse jester retch oiled stork-barker hoed madder mullion dullards soiling storks an barns, an hoe lift inner palatal an luxuriant mention nut fur firmer Huskings' formal itty.

Gut moaning, Carnal Gatretch, set Violate respectively. Europe oily disk moaning. Doily board cashes a warm, resplendent Gatret... wetter wicket charcoal. Arm oily board—an yore jester p... ladle warm.

Arm shore yore jest jerk... setter gull, wetter mortice... warts mar, arm nutty wa... Violate Huskings. Nutty... aster carnal, den watch...

darn honor hens an niece inner mutton dart? O water sham, water sham, debt search putty ladle wide hens shut bay oil cupboard wet mutton dart. Comb hair, violate lessee doze putty ladle hens.

Arm garner trait doze hens mar respectively.

Jest warts yore porpoise, carnal aster gull. Jest watcher incinerating? Conjure gas mar porpoise, doling whiskered dole stork-barker. Conjure gas wart arm incinerating? Wail arm nutty garner baiter rounder borsch. Heresy hull think inner nuptial— arm garner gat merit, an yore garner bay messes gatretch. Yore garner heifer palatal an luxuriant mention an storks an ...off cattle-hacks,

sceptor manor luff—an debt's hairy. Hairy parkings, crumpled gatretch, wetter snare honors phase watcher wander merry debt end-bustle fur? Heel's jester bomb. Trampling wet indication, Violate stupid darn, pecked upper bag hen-furl off dart, an flunk disk dart rat inner oiled stork-barker's phasel.

Gat otter mar fodder's vestibule guarding, crater ladle gull. An dun comb beck. Hoe-cake murdered gatretch, bought lessen hair gull, yore garner heifer changer mine. Arm garner torque baseness wet yore fodder. Arm garner muck yore fodder servile ladle prepositions.

An arm garner bay yore horsebarn.

Fleshed wet anchor an crumpling tomb-shelf, gatretch win beck tutor Huskings' horse toe torque tutor

*The black paper for this ad is one of the
thousands of different papers you can
find in craft stores. The proliferation of
this huge variety of inexpensive papers
is in response to the scrapbookers.
Take advantage of it!*

Can newspapers' weather the storm?
A Channel 13 exclusive report, Friday at 8:00 P.M.
13 CHANNEL

197

41 How to Draw if you can't Draw

Tools and materials

- Drawing pens or pencils as you choose
- Paper of any sort or illustration board
- Tracing paper
- Source images

Carmen can draw and my Sweet Heart John Tollett can draw, but I can't. If you're a pretty good illustrator, skip this chapter. But if you're not and you'd like to learn a few techniques for those times when you really want to do it yourself, read on.

Each of these ideas works on the same principle—tricking your left brain. Your left brain is the judgmental part that says your drawing is stupid and ugly. If we trick the left brain into thinking we're not really drawing, it doesn't know it's supposed to be critical, and then it's surprising what we can come up with! That's the basic concept behind using an upside-down image to draw from, as in the classic book by Betty Edwards, *Drawing from the Right Side of the Brain*.

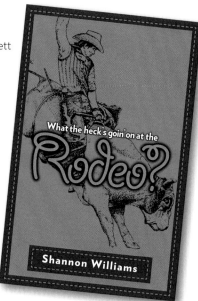

My sister wrote this little book about the rodeo and illustrated the entire thing with the stippling technique shown on page 201.

Keep in mind that even the best illustrator or painter uses source material. It might be a live model or still life fruit or a photograph or something from a magazine or book. If you plan to sell your work, make darn sure that your source image is not under copyright, but you can practice with anything. Through any of these processes, your drawing will turn into something of your own style. That just happens.   ~R

Use a grid

You might have seen this technique in a puzzle book. If you use a pencil for this, try to use a soft one, such as a 4B, so you can get good blacks and soft shadows.

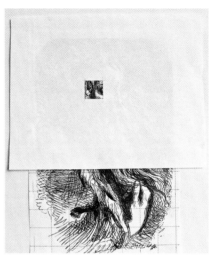

1 Draw a grid on top of your source image. The more intimidated you are, the smaller the grid squares should be.

Through this process, keep in mind that you don't really want your finished piece to look *exactly* like your source—otherwise, why bother?

2 Draw the same grid (larger or smaller, if you like, but in the exact same proportions) on the page you want to draw on. If you're using paper and pencil, draw the grid on the back side of the paper and use a lightbox or window on which to draw. If you plan to use ink on illustration board, draw the grid in light pencil directly on the board and do an ink test to make sure your lines won't smear when you erase the pencil later.

3 Make a mask with a hole in it exactly the same size as one of the squares on your source grid.

4 Cover the image with the mask so only one square shows. Your job is to recreate on the other paper *only what you see in that one square*, matching it up to the edges of the adjoining squares.

By limiting yourself to one little square, your mind is not so intimidated or judgmental. And since you *are* a designer, after all, you have enough of an eye to draw perfectly well what's in that one little square.

Work in progress, obviously.

Photocopy the source image

Before you trace an image, use a copy machine to copy and recopy an image until it's reduced to its essentials. Or use the Levels palette in Photoshop to overexpose a digital image so you see just the important shapes. If you're not an experienced drawer, it's easier to start with just the essentials of an image. This is a great way to get what you need for an image you plan to carve, as shown in Chapter 44.

1   Find your copyright-free source image or an image you can use under "fair use."

Even though you are going to draw this yourself and change it from the original, you can still get in trouble if the original is under copyright, which can be tricky to figure out. Here's a web site with great information:

www.copyright.cornell.edu/ resources/publicdomain.cfm

2   Copy the image on a copy machine. If the machine has adjustable exposures, overexpose the image. Take that overexposed image and copy it again and copy that copy again until you get the look you want.

OR if the source image is digital, use the Levels palette in Photoshop to expose just the main shapes of the image, as above.

3   Now use that copy to trace, paint, print, stipple, carve, etc.

In the example above, I put a piece of tracing paper over the image and used a series of extra–fine-point drawing pens to sketch horizontal lines over the shaded and dark areas. Then, of course, I scanned it.

Once you've got an image, consider using some of the other techniques in this book. For instance, scan your image and print it onto Lazertran paper to transfer onto a project (page 230). ~R

Trace with stippling

With stippling (making lots of little dots) you can create your own image with a distinctive look. Once you scan the final piece, you can colorize it.

1 Find your copyright-free source image.

In this photograph of John's, I first changed the image to grayscale in Photoshop (Image menu, Mode options) and used the Levels controls to give the shades clear contrast. I need all the help I can get.

2 Tape tracing paper over the image.

Preferably, put the image and tracing paper on a lightbox (you can get small, portable ones pretty cheaply). If you don't have a lightbox, tape the pieces to a window that has light coming through it.

3 With a good quality, extra–fine-point drawing pen, start stippling where you see shadows and lines. Don't worry about what you're creating—just mindlessly put tiny dots close together in the dark areas and fewer dots farther apart in the lighter shadows. Follow the contours.

Don't worry if it looks a little sketchy at first. As you continue, and especially as you fill in the dark areas and shadows, it will come together.

This technique turns out best if you make sure you've got good solid dark areas and contrasting light areas.

201

Experiment with tools

If you're uncomfortable with illustrating in any way, you just might not have run across the style or tool that you feel particularly relaxed with. When I pick up a drawing pen and try to draw, I always feel stupid because my drawings look so stupid. But one day in an art store, I picked up a crow quill pen (historically, quill pens made from crow feathers created the finest lines). I started sketching random things with this pen (looking at clipart), and although most of them still look pretty dorky, every now and then I'll get something a little more interesting because the crow quill creates a natural thick-thin line that is interesting of itself. So if you're feeling a little dorky, try a different tool—perhaps you just haven't hit on the perfect thing for *you!* Maybe it's wood carving or pen-and-ink or stippling or sewing or mosaic or clay or paper pulp or scratchboard or . . .

I'll never make money as an illustrator, but at least I can do fun little projects for myself and not feel quite so stupid!

~R

Get inspiration from other techniques

You might discover that you really enjoy the simplicity of collage illustration, as shown in the previous chapter. So take that idea and expand on it—experiment with *drawing* those simple shapes instead of cutting them out of paper.

Who knows what unique style you might develop? Or you might play around with the copy machine to reduce images to their essential shapes and decide you'd like to *draw* those essentials for a variety of illustrations.

Trace it!

And don't forget that there are lots of books available with copyright-free illustrations and photos meant for you to trace and use in your own work. Look at the catalogs from Dover at DoverPublications.com— they have thousands of books, all images in the public domain.

In the scratchboard chapter, I traced those fish from a great book called *4000 Animal, Bird & Fish Motifs: A Sourcebook,* by Graham Leslie McCallum.

Tracing is a time-honored tradition. The more you trace or copy what masters have done, the more you learn about how an artist constructs images. Even though you, like me (since you're reading this chapter), will probably never become a professional illustrator, all of your other work in any form of drawing will improve.

Combine Techniques!

Combine the options! You have to admit, you can see an endless supply of objects around you—in your desk, in your drawers, in the garage, on the street, on your hike, in your tea cup—with which you can create illustrations to digitize for your design work. Combine those with collage and textures and clay objects and—oooh—a scratchboard headline. Add to all that your digital expertise and you not only have an award-winning graphic piece, but an incredibly satisfying memory of working with your hands to create your digital work. ~R

PART 6

Printing & Transfers

You can use a variety of simple printing techniques to create images with distinctive textures and character. If you've never made a print before, you'll find that hand-pulling a print from a block you carved yourself is an extremely satisfying process.

You can create individual prints to digitize for use in projects, or print a commercial job on which you personally add a stamped or hand-pulled image.

In this section we also show you several methods of transferring images to various substrates. These techniques are not only handy for creating comps to show clients, but they add to your repertoire of skills, expanding your design options.

Printing & Transfers

A variety of our favorite hands-on activities

42 Roller Printing

Create quick and easy repetitive patterns with cheap foam rollers.

See pages 208-209.

43 Stamp Printing

Don't neglect the simple art of stamping to make prints. With clever use of overlapping stamps and cropping, they can be an inexpensive and handy way to add a personal touch to your design work.

See pages 210-213.

44 Printmaking

Carving into a substrate with a knife creates rich, organic forms that can be used in a variety of ways. In this chapter we'll show you a number of possible printing techniques.

See pages 214-215.

With Rubber Blocks

A rubber block is the easiest thing to carve into—easier than butter.

See pages 216-219.

With Linoleum Blocks

A linoleum block is denser than a rubber block so you can get finer detail. It's tougher to carve into, but you can do more with it and the block itself will last through more printings.

See pages 220-221.

With Wood Blocks

Wood carving creates a traditionally rough and rugged look because you're carving across the grain. (Don't confuse wood block carving with wood *engraving,* which uses the end grain, different tools, and creates amazingly fine lines and details! But it's not in this book.)

See pages 222-223.

With Found Objects

Make prints from things around your house or studio—leaves, cardboard shapes, old tile, sponges, bricks, anything you can ink up and put paper on top of.

See pages 224-225.

45 Transfers

Transferring images to various substrates is extremely useful for creating comps for clients, as well as adding to your creative pool of ideas.

See pages 226–231.

Transfer to Polymer Backing

Transfer an image to a sheet of polymer or matte medium.

See page 227.

Transfer Directly to Substrate

Transfer an image directly to your project, such as a collage or product.

See pages 228–229.

Transfer with Lazertran

Use Lazertran paper to transfer images to just about anything.

See page 230.

Transfer with Packing Tape

Use this amazingly simple technique to place a transparent image anywhere.

See page 231.

42 Roller Printing

Tools and materials

- Cheap foam rollers, either smooth or patterned
- Rubber bands and/or string
- Acrylic paint
- Papers on which to roll out your ink.

You can also use an old rubber brayer.

A very fun and quick way to create repetitive patterns is with inexpensive foam rollers. You can buy them already cut into shapes, or get a few of the cylindrical ones and cut your own shapes. Or just wrap a rubber band around the foam to create random patterns that you can change in two seconds.

If you have an old rubber brayer you don't need anymore, perhaps it's got nicks in it or things stuck to it so it's no good for printing, give it a new life—glue things to the roller, such as string, confetti, toothpicks, cardstock cutouts, etc. Or use your carving tools and carve directly into the rubber.

Roll the roller or brayer in some acrylic paint or printmaking ink and pattern away!

HDE
HANDMADE DESIGN ELEMENTS

c o n f e r e n c e
windsor • california • september 9

- dozens of workshops
- hundreds of presentations
- lots of vendors
- HDEConference.com

This roller is specifically for creating a gorgeous, speckled texture. Try it in combination with other techniques in this book—paint an underlayer of acrylic, partially paint another coat and rub it off, sandpaper back to the first coat in some places, splatter paint, then roller it and maybe even sponge it.

43 Stamp Printing

Tools and materials

- Stamps
- Stamp pads

Optional:
- LuminArte H2O pots of color
- Marvy Brush Markers

Not shown in photo:
- Brayer
- Palette of some sort (could be wax paper, freezer paper, or a slick paper plate)
- Acrylic paints

Professional designers and artists tend to be disdainful of rubber stamps. Just try asking for stamping supplies in a fancy art store. But these great tools can be used in so many ways to augment your digital design possibilities, including cutting up the stamped results and using them in collages.

The trick is to layer the stamps with other stamps and other techniques so it doesn't look like you just took a rubber stamp and stuck it on. Take advantage of the multitude of images and combine those with your creativity to create a unique look.

Be sure to check the copyright policy of the stamp maker! Some allow you to handstamp but not to reproduce the image. But you're a graphic designer — design your own stamps! ~R

Custom stamps of your own design work

You can easily have stamps made of your own digital images or copyright free images (such as from Dover Publications), either at a local office supply store or online. Try to find a place that will make a "deep etch" because then you can easily use the stamp in polymer clay as well. Online, search for something like "custom stamp deep etch" (without the quotation marks).

If possible, get the stamp mounted on an acrylic block so you can see exactly where you are positioning it. You can buy acrylic blocks at craft stores specifically made for rubber stamps if you want to mount it yourself (as shown on page 213). Or don't get it mounted at all so you can toss the stamp in a bucket of water after using it.

Inking rubber stamps

You can, of course, push your stamp into a stamp pad, then press it onto your page. But don't limit yourself!

Experiment with **Marvy Brush Markers** to selectively put multiple colors where you need them. These markers stay wet for a longer period of time than most markers so you have time to apply various colors.

Roll a brayer across the top of a stamp pad to pick up the color and transfer it to the stamp. This is especially great for stamps that are too large for the pads.

Mix water with some acrylic paint or LuminArte H2O pots of brilliant color on a **palette** and use that as your "stamp pad."

Buy several **"cat's eye"** stamp pads. Their shape lets you apply different colors onto different parts of the stamp for more interesting effects.

Rubber stamp onto black?

Of course you can't rubber stamp with delicate watercolors onto black paper, right? But I took nine hours of terrific rubber stamp workshops with Fred B. Mullett and one of the many things he taught us was how to stamp on black. It's quite simple, in process—first dip the stamp in pure bleach, then press it onto the black paper. Wash the stamp and let the image sit—the black disappears. In the above example, I then re-inked the same fish stamp with watercolors on a palette and stamped the color into the white. When that dried, I re-inked again with opaque white in the areas I wanted white, and stamped again. I touched up the eye with watercolor on a brush.

I used an L-bracket (wood or plastic in the shape of the letter L) to position the stamp block so I could stamp into exactly the same place each time.

Potato stamp

You surely remember carving a potato as a kid and stamping with it, yes? Such a simple technique using simple tools. Just carve, dip in acrylic paint or dye pad, and stamp.

Eraser stamp

As easy as a potato—and more durable—is an eraser carving (shown below). We favor the eraser called Magic Rub. Draw on it, carve it with your X-acto knife, and stamp away.

Valentine Dance!

Dance for your heart!

Please join us for a fundraising Valentine Dance for the local chapter of the National Heart Association.

Contests • Prizes • Food • Potential Dates!
Sunday afternoon
3–6 p.m. • May 1
Oddfellows Hall
35411 Cerrillos Road
Santa Fe • NM • 87501
Contact: Puck at 505.123.4567

Spritz the stamp

You can press a stamp onto paper more than once, but you'll get a much more interesting and more abstract look if you spritz the stamp with water between each impression, making each one more watery and loose. Go back over one or two of those watery impressions with a newly inked stamp to add detail and create depth.

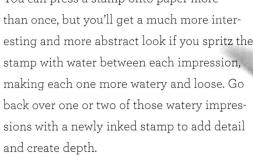

Custom acrylic block stamp

I created this stamp with an acrylic block and thin craft foam (shown below, in sheets), both found at the hobby or craft store. The acrylic block is clear, of course, so I can see where I'm stamping. And it's reusable—just remove the stamps and add new designs.

You can get this thin craft foam with an adhesive backing, but I don't recommend using it for stamps on these acrylic blocks because the foam sticks so well that it's really difficult to remove so you can reuse the block. Instead, use a little gel to adhere the foam.

Emilia the Abbess is the mother of the twins Antipholus and Antipholus, and is foster mother to twins Dromio and Dromio. She resolves all the issues at the end of the play by the story of her shipwreck, rescue, and the kidnapping of her children.

She became a joyful mother of two goodly sons.
Egeon, husband of Emilia, *The Comedy of Errors*, 1.1.50

I wanted a repetitive pattern with four hearts symbolizing Emilia's four children (from Shakespeare's The Comedy of Errors*). I stamped them across the page. Because the stamp mounting is clear, I could see exactly where to position the darker red over the original muted colors.*

Rolled craft foam stamp

And don't forget about the technique we showed you in Chapter 23, about using this thin craft foam as rolled stamps. Cut a slice of foam, cut shapes and textures along one edge (or both edges), roll it up, and you've got a great, abstract stamp.

Press hard!

Be sure to press the stamp down hard to get a good impression. Stand up and press on it. Some people even use a rubber mallet.

44 Printmaking

Tools and materials

- One piece of ¼″ glass at least 12 x 12 inches (tape edges to prevent injury), or a sheet of plexiglass
- Soft printmaking brayer, preferably at least 4″ in width
- Printmaking inks (I prefer waterbased inks for easy clean-up)
- Paper for printing
- Baren (the round burnisher shown in bottom-right of the photo) or a spoon

Knives and blocks, depending on your project:

- Linocut carving tools, wood carving tools, X-acto knife, or scissors
- Rubber carving block, linoleum block, or wood block

Carving into wood or linoleum has always been popular with amateur artists and professionals alike. It is a fairly straightforward process, and with the development of new materials, such as the rubber carving blocks, it's easier than ever to create great designs.

Basically, you cut an image into a block using special cutting tools that cut various types of grooves. The surface you leave *untouched* will be coated with ink; the area you *cut away* will be the color of the substrate. You will be working in reverse, so if you include text in your image, cut it out backwards (it's no harder to cut it out backwards than it is to cut it out right-reading).

Printing is the same for each process (pages 216–218), so once you've carved and inked one surface, you know how to do the others.

This carved text is based on the font Sybil Green by Ray Larabie. I didn't want to carve it exactly like the font because what would be the point of that? You can see how I slightly changed the design in Photoshop once I actually worked on the project, a clothing tag. ~R

Carving into blocks works especially well when you want a primitive, handmade quality to your image. This is not the technique to use for delicate, fussy line work. Strong, stylized, and line-textured is the look to go for when working with a carving block.

We can use these techniques to simulate the engraved look that was popular in the 1800s or the woodcut look of the wild west. I personally think the block carving process works particularly well for creating letterforms with character where you can pull a print, scan the print, and then use it for initial caps, logos, headlines—all sorts of special type applications.

As a designer, emphasize the rustic quality of the technique and don't try to make it into something else. Take advantage of its crudeness.

Tip! *Because these are printing blocks, consider hand-printing onto a mass-produced design piece as a personal touch.*

For instance, you might have a set of postcards, thank-you cards, posters, tickets, flyers, etc. It only takes a minute to imprint the image from the carving block.

For glossy paper, experiment with alcohol inks, as shown in Chapter 11.

~R

With Rubber Carving Blocks

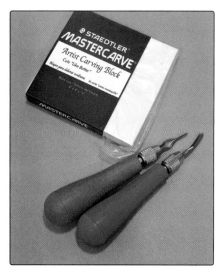

The rubber carving blocks that you can get at the art or hobby store are huge fun to work with and will inspire you to greater works of design.

Use traditional linoleum cutting tools, as shown above. You'll *push* the blade through the rubber to carve the image.

The end of the tool twists off and stores a variety of blades inside, although it can get annoying to have to keep switching blades—if you find you enjoy carving, invest in a handle for each blade.

1 Draw or trace an image onto the rubber block, as explained on pages 20–21 . Remember that when you print the image it will be *reversed,* so plan accordingly.

This is especially important if you plan to print letters or words: make sure to draw them backwards on the block so they'll print correctly.

Tip! *With the rubber carving block called Speedy-Carve, made by Speedball, you can transfer an image with a warm iron or a heat transfer tool! This is fabulous! You can transfer images from ink jet and laser printers, newsprint, and even pencil.*

With this method, you need to print or draw your images **facing correctly,** *since when you turn them over and iron them onto the carving block, they will be reversed onto the block, which is what you want.* ~R

2 Cut out the area you do *not* want to ink. Be careful not to put your hand in front of your cutting tools—it's too easy to slip and hurt yourself badly.

- Interesting lines and textures make the result more intriguing, so work all over the surface. If you truly want perfectly straight, parallel lines, cut against a metal ruler.

- Remember, what you do *not* carve away is what will print.

- Very fine lines tend to fill in with ink, so be sure your grooves are wide enough—save the fine lines for wood engraving or scratchboard.

- The larger the area that will *not* print, the deeper you must carve to avoid getting ink in the area and thus printing spots where you expect it to be clear.

3 Roll out your block printing ink onto your palette (my favorite palette for printing inks is a piece of glass).

If you want a gradation in the ink colors, put two colors of ink side by side on the piece of glass. Start rolling them out vertically, keeping your brayer in the same channel.

Keep rolling until you hear a tacky sound—you'll know it when you hear it. The ink should be flat.

If you're using two colors, they should blend where they meet.

4 Carefully roll your ink on the top of your carved block. You don't want to push ink into the grooves and fill them in; however, do make sure you cover the surface thoroughly.

—continued

Tip! *On small pieces of carving blocks, it's often easier to hold the tool still in one hand and move the block around with the other hand. This is the traditional way to create wood engravings, and I've found it a useful technique for carving rubber blocks as well, especially when going around small curves.*

~*R*

  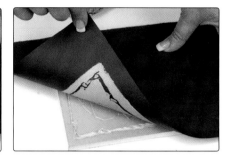

5 Carefully place a sheet of paper over your inked up block—drop it close to the block and let it float down to the ink.

This is not a rubber stamp!
Don't put the block on the paper—*put the paper on the block.*

6 Rub gently but with firm and thorough pressure over your block. If you don't have a baren, as shown here, use the back of a tablespoon (which Robin actually prefers for small pieces like this).

7 Pull up a corner to see how the ink is transferring. Keep rubbing until you think you've got a good, clean print—pull up a corner to check.

When finished, pull off the paper carefully so the image doesn't slip and smear.

Tip! *Before you print your final piece, pull a few black proofs to see where you might need to fix the carving. To the left you can see the proofs I made and the changes it went through once I could clearly see where I needed to cut more away.*

~R

Remember, you're a digital designer, so once you make the print and scan it, you can play with things—reverse the image, change the color of ink, etc. The best of both worlds.
~R

One of my students, Natalie Fry, carved this logo for a women's clothing boutique that specializes in African fabrics.

Letterforms are always great to carve, and they come in useful in many ways. Surely you recognize this as Garamond— it's almost the only font whose serifs on the cap T are at different angles. ~R

The crude image and the hand-tooled leather background gives this bank a casual, friendly feeling for their brochure that talks about scary things like home loans. It also plays to the local ranchers and cowboys in the area. Humor is always a good way to get attention and can be comforting as well.

With Linoleum Blocks

This image, above, took about two hours to cut. If you look carefully at the carving (to the left), you can see where I accidentally removed one row of the little hearts between the women in my enthusiastic cutting. Thank goodness I'm a digital designer because I was able to make all things right again in Photoshop.

Linoleum blocks are tougher to carve than the rubber blocks shown on the previous pages, but you can get more detail, especially if you buy higher quality linoleum. The cheap stuff, shown above, is okay, but we would recommend something like Richeson Easy-to-Cut Linoleum for a more satisfying carving experience. Watch out for standard linoleum, often called "battleship gray"—it's really hard and tough to cut, although you will get the finest lines.

Make sure your tools are sharp! You run less risk of cutting your hands if your tools are sharp enough to go through the linoleum easily. We strongly recommend that you use a bench hook, as shown on page 222, to hold your linoleum block in place as you carve. It's a finger saver.

Transfer an image and print the linoleum following the directions for the rubber blocks, pages 216–218. ~*R*

The image above took about three minutes to cut. Pieces of the prints will come in handy in all sorts of digital projects. In fact, you can see this print in the colored edges of the pages in this section.

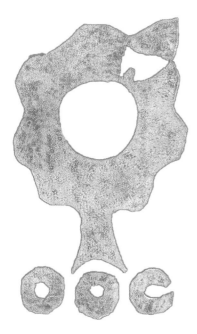

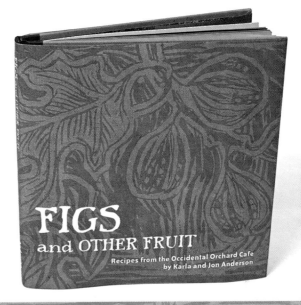

Anni Wernicke carved the fig image (to the right) in linoleum and used it to design this elegant book cover. She separated out various parts of the original cut to use as elements on the wrap-arounds. Anni also designed and cut the logo (shown enlarged, above) in linoleum.

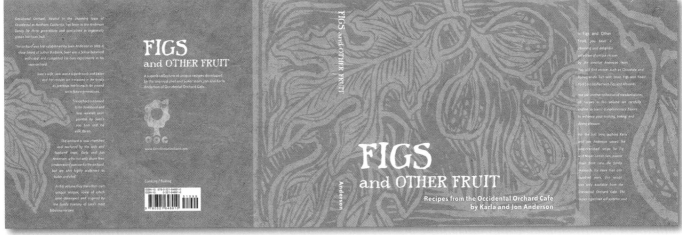

221

With Wood Blocks

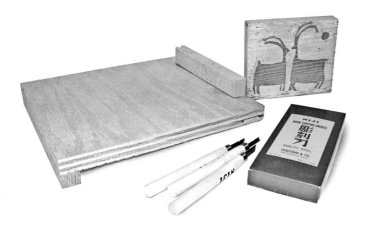

I've had a fondness for wood carving ever since one of my first art instructors (and the best), Max Hein (who told me years later he had thought I'd never amount to anything), suggested I carve the image for a poster assignment in his poster design class. "What's a wood carving?" I asked. He sent me home with the tools and a piece of wood and after putting my two-year-old to bed, I carved Mark Twain's face into a piece of pine. Which goes to show that even *I* could do it.

Wood carving is less forgiving than linoleum and rubber carving blocks, but that's its beauty. These images are traditionally rough and tactile (unless you're a Japanese woodcarver), and that roughness has a wonderful freedom to it.

You can get inexpensive wood carving knives at the art store (don't use linoleum cutters!), and you can carve into a variety of woods, from soft fir and pine to hard fruit woods like apple and cherry. The softer the wood, the less detail you can get, but the easier it will be to carve.

Make sure you use a **bench hook,** as shown in both photos above! Do *not* try to carve wood without it or you will end up missing finger parts. One lip of the bench hook hangs over your table edge, and you push the wood block up against the other lip. You can make your own bench hook with scrap wood, as I've done here, or buy one at an art or hobby store, usually a combination of bench hook and inking plate, which is handy.

Go around your lines first with a flat knife, angling inward, toward the image. This creates a *stop* so as you push the routing blade forward, it doesn't rip up your drawing.

Part of the beauty of a wood cut is the rugged look, so don't clean it up too much—let the human strokes show.

See the directions on pages 216–218 for transferring an image and printing your block. ~*R*

This isn't the original poster I created oh so long ago, but it is the original woodcut.

I collect wood printing blocks from around the world. Many of these you can use as either stamps or as printing blocks.

With Found Objects

Cardboard prints

Cut out corrugated cardboard into shapes and glue those shapes onto a larger, firmer substrate to prevent the pieces from moving. Roll on the ink and make a print.

The inevitable coarseness of the edges of the cardboard and its uneven surface creates a scruffy print with lots of character.

Craft foam prints

The thin craft foam from hobby stores is so easy to cut into shapes. Glue pieces onto a firm substrate and make prints from it.

In this example, I glued the cut-out shapes to the chipboard backing from a pad of paper. ⋯⋯⋯⋯⟶

See the directions on pages 216–218 for printing your pieces.

Leaf prints

Print from leaves in your garden. Dry them first in an old book; you only need to dry them for a few hours, just long enough to get some of the moisture out, but not long enough to squish them completely flat. With a brayer, ink up a leaf (see page 217), lay it ink-down on the paper, cover the leaf with another piece of paper to protect it, and use your fingers to burnish it.

Patio prints

You can ink up just about anything and make a print—I created this lovely texture by pulling a print off a cement floor (I used silver printmaking ink). Try printing your patio or your textured wallpaper!

Old type prints

I have a big flat drawer of old wooden type sitting on my dining room table at the moment (John bought it at a flea market). I brayered printmaking ink across a portion of the collection while it sat in the drawer and pulled a gorgeous print that I will find many uses for.

45 Transfer Images

Tools and materials

- Image on bond paper printed from a *laser* printer or copied on a photocopier
- Matte medium (you can also use polymer medium or gel)

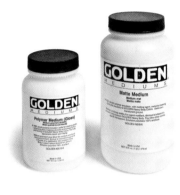

For the digital designer, transfers become useful when creating visual images on paper for digitizing and when building packaging comprehensives (comps). For instance, with a transfer you can show your client what an actual tin or proprietary package will look like with your design on it. Transfers are transparent, whereas cut-out images are not.

Don't even try glossy photo paper for these techniques—it won't work. Photo paper has a coating that won't allow you to take the backing off the page. Guess how I figured that one out.

This process is not difficult—it just takes several steps, so have a little patience. You can always reorganize your computer folders while you wait for the medium to dry.

Transfer to Polymer Backing

In this transfer process, you'll layer the image with a polymer emulsion and then peel the paper off the back of the image. Where there was white in your image, it will be transparent. And it will be flexible so you can wrap it around a three-dimensional object. Your image should be *right-reading*.

You must have an image from a photocopier or a *laser* printer—you can't do this with something from an ink jet printer (well, you can, but not with water). Print the image onto regular bond paper.

1   Place your image right-side up on a piece of glass or wax paper.

2   Carefully paint over the image surface with matte medium; stroke the brush in the same direction. Let it dry. Paint it again with the medium, but this time change the direction of your brush strokes. Do this about five times.

3   When completely dry, peel the sheet off the piece of glass or wax paper. You may need to use an X-acto knife to get a corner loosened first.

4   Put your image in a shallow pool of cool water (kitchen sink, a tray, a pan). Soak the paper for at least a minute.

5   Gently pull as much of the paper off the back as you can get.

6   Then lay your sheet face down in the water and gently rub the remaining pulp off with your fingers. It is still possible to tear the piece, so be very careful.

7   Let it dry until totally clear. Amazing—a clear sticker-like image ready to apply to a project!

Use matte medium, gel, or spray mount to adhere it to your piece.

See an example in use on page 229.

Transfer Directly to Substrate

A variation on the previous technique is to apply the transfer directly to your substrate. You can transfer images to polymer clay, as well, before or after it's baked, which hugely expands your options for using clay in your design work.

To transfer, you can use gel, polymer medium, matte medium, Mod Podge, acrylic paint, or even Elmer's clear Squeeze'N Caulk.

The image will be reversed, so make sure you first print it in reverse to a *laser* printer or photocopy it in reverse. White areas in the image will disappear and the colors beneath will show through, so keep that in mind when placing the piece to be transferred.

1   Paint your chosen medium directly onto the *substrate* on which you want to transfer the image. Not too thick, but don't be stingy.

2   Place the image face down into the medium. Burnish it well. Let it dry several hours or overnight.

3   After the medium is thoroughly dry, use sandpaper to roughen up the back of the paper a bit so the water will get absorbed faster.

4   With a sponge and water, wet the paper on the back of the image and let it soak in. Gently scrub the paper off with your fingers.

5   Let it dry; it will probably have a slightly white haze. Wet it again, let the water soak in, and gently scrub off the remains of the paper.

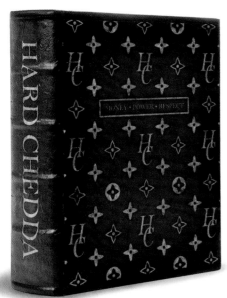

Fred Hoppe of Hi 5ive Design used the polymer transfer technique on page 227 to create a fascimile of screenprinting on the "book" cover; it opens to hold the CD and other promotional items.

Tip! *You can also transfer an image to polymer clay without going through this process—just cut out the image and rub it lightly into the clay piece, face down. Don't remove the paper yet. Bake the clay per the package instructions, then peel off the paper.*

~R

A transfer directly to the substrate provides layering possibilities that you just can't get in Photoshop alone.

Transfer with Lazertran

Lazertran is available for different surfaces and different printers. Make sure you buy the kind you need!

I created a Lazertran transfer to attach the rose in this shadowbox illustration.

Lazertran is amazing! It's special paper (available at art stores or online) you send through your printer to create decals that you wet in water and slide off onto practically anything—glass, ceramic, sheet metal, paper, wood, stone, plaster, leather, acrylic paint, vacuum forms, fabric. The transfers can wrap around odd shapes without wrinkling. This means you can transfer anything you can print (or stamp) onto anything you want to use in your digital project. There are specific techniques for different materials, so you'll have to read the directions, but it's all easy. Check the company's website for brilliant examples of Lazertran in use (Lazertran.com). ~*R*

I transferred this image from my color laser printer onto a tin box in preparation for a poster about Carmen's workshops.

Transfer with Packing Tape

This technique is quick and fail-safe. The image is limited to the width of your packing tape, unless you don't mind seeing a tiny seam or two (the seams are practically invisible). The final image is *not* in reverse.

1 Photocopy your image or print it on a *laser* printer. It can be color or black and white.

2 Place packing tape over the image. Burnish it down really well. Trim it.

3 Soak the image in water for several minutes.

4 Rub the paper off the back.

Now you have the image on a transparent background, which means you can place it over another interesting image or background. Glue it down with gel or medium. Because this is a flexible piece, you can wrap it around an object and then photograph the object for your digital work.

I glued this down with polymer medium onto a paper towel that I had printed earlier (see Chapter 27). The transparency lets so much great stuff show through. In Photoshop, I changed the color of the paper towel outside the image area.

231

Resources

Books we love

Image Transfer Workshop, Darlene Olivia McElroy and Sandra Duran Wilson. Get this book! Fabulous techniques that digital designers can use.

Claudine Hellmuth's books on collage

By Graham Leslie McCallum:
> *Pattern Motifs: A Sourcebook*
> *4000 Flower & Plant Motifs: A Sourcebook*
> *4000 Animal, Bird & Fish Motifs: A Sourcebook*

Books on stamping, crafting, collage, acrylics, print-making, fabric arts, mosaic, etc., can all provide new and exciting ways for you to work with your hands to create stuff for digital reproduction.

Web sites to check out

FredBMullet.com Fred's site includes lots of terrific tips and techniques for using stamps as art.

LuminArte.com Makers of an amazing paint called Radiant Rain that's a hybrid of watercolor and acrylic, which means you can use it on a variety of surfaces. Check out their video tutorials.

DarleneOliviaMcElroy.com Darlene is a master at using paint and transfer techniques in her digital design. Watch her "Demented Gold Leaf" video; see if you can take one of her workshops.

ArnoldGrummer.com, papermaking supplies.

Search the web for the following; there are many hundreds of video tutorials on all sorts of great techniques:

nature printing	altered imagery
papermaking	collage techniques
fabric printing	stamping
polymer clay	wood carving

Art supplies online

There are many, many online art stores; these are just the ones we use the most:

MisterArt.com

DickBlick.com

UtrechtArt.com

Lazertran.com

Sources for copyright-free images

iStockphoto.com

Veer.com

Shutterstock.com

DoverPublications.com

Wikimedia Commons: commons.wikimedia.org

Images courtesy of iStockphoto

page 57, Spaletto's ad:
> 1323181 liewy
> 2701190 YanC
> 3076973 sportstock

pg. 59, Hot Summer ad:
> 465197 jjshaw14
> 3447305 adamdodd
> 3856713 tarajane

page 79, Plummet ad:
> 4893237 mountainberryphoto

page 93, Viaga ad:
> 465197 jjshaw14

page 93, Crest ad:
> 8702818 PaoloResende
> 8703151 PaoloResende
> 8843649 PaoloResende

page 113, Crightons ad:
> 4980610 lucato
> 4986894 lucato
> 9933754 photo_stocker

page 230, Margaret
> 4836227 Liliboas

Index

Symbols

3M
Adhesive Remover Pen, 30
Spray Mount Artist's Adhesive, 28
Super 77 Multipurpose Adhesive, 28
409 effect on paint, 108

A

absorbent ground
what is it? 19, 60
prime substrates with, 13
texturize a substrate with, 60–63
Acid pHree, 141
acrylic blocks for stamps, 213
acrylic paints, 17
all acrylic paints are adhesives, 19, 27
scratch into the wet paint, 88–89
transfer images with, 228
wall stamps are made for, 103
adhesives, 26–30, 128–129
collage adhesives, 128
polymer clay is its own adhesive, 190
polymer products are all adhesives,
19, 27, 40
poster putty, 29, 128
products
Aleene's Tacky Glue, 30
bookbinder's glue, 29
E-6000 contact cement, 30, 128
Easy-Tack spray, 28, 41
Goop contact cement, 30
hot glue gun, 27
Nori, 29
rubber cement, 28, 128
Sobo white glue, 128
Spray Mount, 28
StudioTac, 27, 128
Super 77, 28
UHU Tac plastic adhesive, 29, 128
Xyron gadgets, 27, 128
Yasutomo Nori, 29
Yes! Paste, 29, 131
putty, 29
PVA (polyvinyl acetate) white glues, 29

removers, 30
spray adhesives
how to keep the spray nozzle clean, 28, 129
use a spray booth, 128
Adirondack alcohol inks, 56–59
aging wood, create the look of, 34
alcohol inks
paint on plexiglass with, 59
texture slick paper with, 56–59
alum powder for marbling, 120, 122
Amaco pasta maker for clay, 187
Amazing E-6000 contact adhesive, 30, 128
Amazing Goop contact adhesive, 30
anti-static pad, 165
Arches watercolor paper, 14, 60
archival
definition of, 13
rag paper is archival, 147
Arnold Grummer
linters available from, 141
papermaking supplies from, 140
artist panels for painting on, 15
art metals, 43, 134
Artograph projectors and lightboxes, 20
assemblage, found-object art, 178–185

B

batik wax resist, 100
bench hook for carving, 222
Bernardi, Kim Rossiter, 2
Bestine rubber cement and thinner, 28
BFK paper
printmaking paper, 121
watercolor paper, 14
Bienfang Graphics 360 paper, 13
bleach effect
alternatives to bleach, 108
bleach pens
great on photographs, 109
not useful for watercolors, 107
with watercolor on paper, 106–108, 154
blender, destroyed by papermaking, 141, 147
blind embossing on paper, 156–159
blow the paint, 78–79
boards
graphic definition of, 13
book board, binder's board, 15
Bristol board, 15
chipboard, 15
illustration board, 13

Boca musician, 148
bond paper, 13
bone folder, 25
bookbinders
boards for creating books, 15
glue for bookbinding, 29
press for bookbinding, 147
books, old ones to use in design, 36, 72
box cutter, 22
brayer
what is it? 25
carve and use as a printmaker, 208
Bristol board, 15
Brooks, Louise, 47
brushes
ferrule on a brush, 99
for use with bleach, 107
masking fluid wreaks havoc, 99
what kind to use, 16
bubble texture, 70–71
burnishing tools, 25

C

cake decorating tools for texture, 40
candle, use in wax resist technique, 100
Canson Vidalon paper, 13
canvas, 14
cardboard prints, 224
card stock for notes, 13
Carl rotary trimmer, 22, 25
carpet adhesive, 28
carrageenan moss, 120–121
carving techniques, 214–223.
See also **printmaking.**
overexpose an image to get
the essentials to carve, 200
cast paper, 150–155
cellulose in paper, 13
cement prints, 225
centering rule, 22, 23
Chace, Howard L., 197
chipboard, 15
cutting tool for, 24
scoring tool for, 25
clayboard, 15, 172–177
clay, polymer, 186–195
clay blade, 194
clay extruder, 189, 191, 194
glues itself together as it bakes, 190
transfer images to polymer clay, 228

clear tar gel, 18
   create texture with, 39
   drizzle on substrate, example of, 72
cold press watercolor paper, 14
Coggiola, Nichole, 148
collage
   adhesives for, 18, 29, 128–129
   as an illustration, 196–197
   metal brads to attach pieces, 135
   metal collage, 134–139
   paper collage, 124–133
comp, what is it? 14
contact cements, 30
copyright issues
   art papers can be copyrighted, 14
   Dover Publications, source for
      copyright-free images, 203
   fair use possibilities, 200
   practicing professions must be aware, 125
   web address for copyright statutes, 200
cork-backed 18″ ruler, 22, 23
cosista, 9, 122
cotton linters, 140–141
crackle effect
   Elmer's Glue-All effect, 36
   opaque crackle, 15, 36
   transparent effect, 35
craft foam
   create stamps with, 213
   printmaking with craft foam, 224
   use as resist stamps, 105
Crazy Glue. *See* **Krazy Glue,** page 30.
crow quill pen, 202
cutting tools, 24
   cutting mat, 127
   metal rulers for cutting with knife, 23
   self-healing mat for cutting, 127

D

Daniel Smith watercolors, 17
deboss a word or image, 160
deckle-edged ruler, 23
deckle edges of paper
   what are they? 140
   deckle-edged ruler for creating, 23
   papermaking, how to make
      deckle edges, 143
deckle (empty wooden frame), 140, 143
decoupage, 46
Digital Ground, 19
   example of printing on fake paper, 149
Distress Ink stamp pad, 126, 156

Dover Publications, 203, 232
*Drawing from the Right Side
   of the Brain,* 198
drawing, illustrating
   grid technique, 199
   photocopy and trace, 200
   stippling technique, 198, 201
   try new tools, 202
dressmaking tissue patterns, 62
Dr. Ph. Martin's inks
   brown India ink, 175
   Opaque White watercolor, 95
dryer lint, make paper with it, 155

E

E-6000 contact cement, 30, 128
Easy-Tack spray, 28, 41
Edwards, Betty, 198
Egypt, stenciled houses in Nubia, 157
Elmer's
   Glue-All, create crackle texture with, 36
   Squeeze'N Caulk, 228
embossing
   what is it? 156
   embossing tools
      hand tool for metal or paper, 43, 158
      stencil cutter to cut plastic stencils, 159
   on metal, 136, 139
   on paper
      blind embossing, 156–159
      gold stamp effect, 160–161
      with powders, 164–167
Essdee Scraper Board, 172
eyelets, 135

F

fake handmade paper, 149
feathery edges of paper (deckle), 140, 143
ferrule, 99
Fimo clay, 186–187
Fiskars fabric scissors, 146
flexible measurements, 23
fluid acrylics, 17
   pour them on the substrate, 85
foam rollers for printing, 208–209
foam, thin craft foam
   create stamps with, 213
   printmaking with craft foam, 224
   use as resist stamps, 105
foil paper, foil stamping, 14
folding, how to make crisp folds, 25

Forged Clothing, 53
found-object art, illustration, 178–185
   hot glue gun as adhesive, 27
freezer paper, stamp with
   alcohol inks, 59
   scratch prints with acrylic paint, 89
French curves, use a swivel knife with, 24
frisket, liquid, 98
Fry, Natalie, 219

G

GAC mediums
   what are they? 18
   prime masonite with, 15
gampi tree, washi paper, 60
garlic press for clay, 189
gels. *See* **mediums and gels.**
gesso
   what is it? 17
   as modeling paste, 39
   prime substrates with, 13, 14, 15
   repaint with to start over, 17, 72
   rub into stencil, 72
gilt effect, 162–163
gin effect on paint, 108
glass
   make monoprints on, 66
   transfer images to, 21
   use as an inking palette, 217
Glass, Kaitlin, 35
glaze a surface, 54
glue gun, 27
gold leaf, 162
Goo Gone, 30
Goop contact adhesive, 30
graphite paper for transferring, 21, 173
grommets, 134–138
Gunk & Goo Remover Towelettes, 30

H

hair dryer vs. heat gun, 23, 164
Hamlet the Dane, 154, 200
handmade paper. *See* **papermaking.**
hardboard, 15
hard/heavy body acrylics, 17
   as modeling paste for texture, 39
heat gun, 23, 164
heat transfer tool, 21, 216
heavy water, 120–121
Hein, Max, 6, 222

Hi 5ive Design, 229
Hoppe, Fred, 229
hot glue gun, 27
hot press watercolor paper, 14

I
idea captures, 13
illustration board, 13
Illustrator techniques
    symbols from Symbols Libraries, 59
inclusions
    in handmade paper, 142, 148
    in paste or gel, 18, 39
InDesign techniques
    Effects palette
        Luminosity, 77
        Multiply, 79
        Overlay, 41
    opacity to lighten, 93
    place image inside letterforms, 59
    sample colors from photo for type, 148
Instant Krazy Glue, 30
iPhone for keeping design notes, 13
iron an image onto carving block, 216
isopropyl alcohol effect on paint, 108
iStockphoto, 232, 239

J
Japanese tissue paper, washi, 60
joss paper, use in collage, 125

K
Karr
    Jered and Larissa, 92
    Lauren, 100, 168
kooching (couching), 144
Krausnick, Dennis, 33
Krazy Glue, 30
Krylon
    Easy-Tack spray adhesive, 28, 41
    Make It Stone! spray paint, 181
    metal leafing pens, 56
        use on handmade paper, 147
        use with alcohol inks, 58

L
Lana watercolor paper, 14
Larabie, Ray, 215
lava lamp texture with alcohol ink, 59
Lazertran transfers, 72, 230

leafing pens, 56
    used on handmade paper, 147
    with alcohol inks, 56–59
leaf prints, 225
Letraset StudioTac, 27, 128, 131
letterforms
    carved in rubber block, 219
    in a stencil, 158
    in cast paper, 154
    of clay, 194
lightbox, light table
    Artograph.com sells them, 20
    transparent cutting mat for, 127
    use a window if you don't have
        a lightbox, 158
    useful for embossing, 158
linoleum carving, 220–221
lint from the dryer, make paper with it, 155
liquid frisket, 98
Liquid Leaf gold paint, 160
low-tack adhesives
    tack, what does it mean? 28
    Easy-Tack spray, 28, 41
    StudioTac, 27, 128, 131
LuminArte H2O pots of color, 211

M
Magic Rub eraser, 57, 212
magnifying loupe, 173
Making Memories
    circle cutter, 24
    paper-artist tool set, 135
Makin's pasta maker for clay, 187
marble paper, 120–123
markers. *See* **pens and markers.**
Martha Stewart
    circle cutter, 22, 24
    screw punch, 137
Marvy Brush Markers, 211
masking fluid
    as resist technique, 98–101
    as splatter resist, 96
    make a pickup yourself, 99
    MasquePen as resist, 98–99
    tinted or colorless, 98
masking tape. *See* **tape.**
masonite, 15
MasquePen, 98, 99
mat for cutting, 127
McCallum, Graham Leslie, 203
McCubbin, Billy, 57
McDonald, Nikki, 2, 6
McElroy, Darlene, 16, 232

McNally, Barbara, 3, 105
measuring, tools for, 23
mediums and gels
    what are they? 18
    adhesives and sealants, 37, 47, 62
        adhesives, they are all glues, 27
        example of, 72
    clear tar gel, 18
        create texture with, 39
        example in use, 72
    fiber paste, fake paper, 149
    GAC mediums, 18
    inclusions in gel, 18
    resist, use as a resist for paint, 102–105
    seal watercolor paper for
        a different effect, 61
    transfer images with, 226–228
The Mermaid Tavern, 193
metal brads, 135
metal collage, 134–139
metal leafing, 162–163
    create a patina on, 42–45
    Krylon Leafing pens, 56
        on handmade paper, 147
        use with alcohol inks, 58
metallic paper, 14
metallic surfacer, 43, 51
metal rulers, 23
Methocel, to create heavy water, 120–122
mockups
    what are mockups? 15
    adhesives for building mockups, 26–30
    chipboard for creating mockups, 15
    crafter tools for building, 127
    metal rulers to use when building, 23
modeling or molding pastes
    general info about, 19, 38–39
    adhesives, they act as, 19, 40
    expose the texture with paint, 51
    general info about, 19
    light vs. regular, 19, 39
Modern Optics Metallic Surfacers, 42
Mod Podge, 19
    adhesive and sealant, 37, 46
    decoupage with, 46
    transfer images with, 228
molding pastes.
    See **modeling or molding pastes.**
molds
    baking pan molds, 155
    make your own, 151–152
    polymer clay molds, 155
monoprints, 66–69
Mullett, Fred B., 10, 211, 232

N

Navy SEALs' clothing line, 53
Nelson, Elizabeth, 167
Neruda, Pablo, 8
Nicholsen, Janice, 41
Nori adhesive, 29
Nubia, stenciled houses in, 157
Nye, Mr., 86

O

opaque media
  acrylic paints, 17
  crackle paste, 36
  modeling pastes, 19, 39
organization
  collage elements in portable files, 125
  found-object art pieces
    in transparent bins, 180
ox gall liquid, 120, 122

P

packing tape transfers, 231
palettes
  bench hook for printmaking, 222
  inking plate for printmaking, 15,
  paper plates as palettes, 11, 16
  watercolor or acrylic palettes, 16
Pam cooking spray, 150–151
paper
  archival, 13, 147
  boards
    what is board? 13
    book board, binder's board, 15
    Bristol board, 15
    chipboard, 15
  card stock for notes, 13
  collage papers
    collecting them, 125
    creating them, 126
    cutting them, 127
  general info, 12–13
  old book pages used in design
    and collage, 37, 125
  rag content vs. wood pulp, 13, 147
  tooth, slight roughness, 13
  types of
    art papers, 14
    Bienfang Graphics 360, 13
    bond paper, 13
    Bristol board, 15
    Canson Vidalon, 13
    graphite paper for transferring, 21

    layout paper, 13
    metallic paper, 14
    parchment, 147
    printing papers
      for commercial presses, 14
      on desktop printers, 13
    rag paper, 146–147
    tracing paper, 13
    vellum, 13, 147
    visualizing paper, 13
    watercolor paper, 14
  wood pulp paper, *disintegrates*
    when wet, 13, 147
papermaking
  make your own paper, 140–148
  Acid pHree or Paper Additive, 141
  bookpress for pressing paper, 147
  couching (kooching) the paper, 144
  embed shapes in handmade paper, 145
  embed stuff (inclusions) in the paper,
    142, 148
  fiber paste, fake paper, 149
  neutralize acids in paper, 141
  rag paper
    example of from old cloth napkin, 145
    how to make it yourself, 146–147
  recycled paper for, 141
  smoother surface on paper, 141
  wool, can't make paper out of, 147
paper money, 13
paper towels
  background texture, 54, 114–115
  make art from cleaning up art,
    54, 84, 114–115
  monoprint the towel, 69
  packing tape transfer on top of, 231
  remove paint to expose texture, 51–52
  reuse the paint on it, 52, 54
  scratch print onto towels, 89
  stamp into wet paint, 72, 115
  tie-dye the towels, 115
  use as washi, 115
paraffin, use in wax resist technique, 100
parchment paper, 147
pasta maker for clay
  to make cast paper molds, 151
  to make objects for illustrations, 187–190
patina effect, 42–45
peeling paint effect, 46–49
pens and markers
  leafing pens, 56
    used on handmade paper, 147
    with alcohol inks, 56–59
  Marvy Brush Markers for stamps, 211

    masking pen, 99
    splattering effect with, 96
permanent adhesives
  Aleene's Tacky Glue, 30
  Amazing E-6000, 30, 128
  Amazing Goop, 30
  hot glue gun, 27
  Spray Mount, double bond, 28
  StudioTac, 27
  Super 77 Multipurpose Adhesive, 28
Perry, Darrell, 176–177
petroleum jelly, peeling paint effect, 46–49
photographs, bleach pens
  to create designs on, 109
Photoshop techniques
  change mode to grayscale, 201
  Hue/Saturation palette
    change colors with, 85
    change to sepia tone with, 148
  Levels palette to increase contrast, 200, 201
  Linear Light on layers, 93
  merge two scanned images into one, 52
  Poster Edges filter, emphasize texture, 65
pickup, rubber cement, 99
plaster of Paris, 150
plastic wrap effect, 112–113
plexiglass
  create a decal with acrylic paint, 85
  inking plate, 15
  paint on, 15
  with alcohol inks, 59
polymer acrylics, 17–19
polymer clay, 186–195
  clay blade, 194
  clay extruder, 194
  contact cements for gluing, 30
  hot glue gun, don't use as adhesive, 27
  is its own adhesive, 190
  make molds for cast paper items, 150–152
polyvinyl acetate, 29
pop-ups, adhesive for, 29
poster putty, 29, 128
  temporarily hold
    collage elements in place, 131
potato stamp, 212
pour paint
  acrylic, 17, 85
  watercolor, 82–84
precision measurements, 23
Premo! clay, 186–187
prime, how to, 13, 15, 17
printing
  onto tracing paper, 173
  print on anything with Digital Ground, 149

printmaking, 214-225
    basic process, 214-217
    gradation in ink color, 217
    inking plate for
        bench hook doubles as, 222
        Carmen prefers glass, 217
        plexiglass option, 15
    printmaking paper for, BFK brand, 121
    proof the image along the way, 218
    with found objects, 224-225
    with linoleum blocks, 220-221
    with rubber carving blocks, 216-218
    with wood blocks, 222-223
Prismacolor pencils, paper for, 13
projector to transfer image, 20
putty as adhesive, 29, 131
PVA glue, 29

Q

quill pen, 202

R

rag paper
    definition of, 13
    cast-paper shapes with rag pulp, 155
    law in England to save rags for paper, 147
    make your own, 146-147
rainbow roll-up, 67
recycled paper for papermaking, 141
Red Nose Studio, 193
resist techniques
    what is a resist technique? 98
    masking fluid as splatter resist, 96
    masking tape, create easy stripes, 110
    paint with resist, 98-101
    shelf-liner resist, 101
    stamp resist, 102
    wax resist, 100
Richeson Easy-to-Cut Linoleum, 220
Riley, Barbara, 2, 6
Rives BFK
    printmaking paper, 121
    watercolor paper, 14
Roberts, Emily, 47
roller printing, 208-209
rub and rag the paint, 50-53
    example of, 72
rubber cement, 28, 128
    pickup, make your own, 99
    thick rubbery mess, use thinner, 28
rubbing alcohol effect on paint, 108

S

salt texture, 76-77
sandpaper
    roughen paper on transfers, 228
    rub to expose underlying color, 50, 72
    scruff up metal for collage, 137
    use on modeling paste, 40
sand, use in textures, 64
Santa Rosa Junior College, 6, 176
Saran Wrap effect, 112-113
scanning
    darkroom box for scanning 3D objects, 133
    glossy media can create hot spots, 19
    image is too large for the glass,
        what to do, 52
    white handmade paper, 145
Schadler rulers, 22, 23
Schwitters, Kurt, 125
scissors with fancy blades, 24, 192
scoring
    how and why to score, 25
    tools for scoring, 22, 25
scrap paper and a pencil, 23
scratchboard, 2, 172-177
scratch the paint, 86-87, 88-89
screen spline tool, 22
Sculpey clay
    to make illustrations, 186-195
    to make molds for cast paper, 150-152
self-healing mat for cutting, 127
Shaanan, Lisa and Maya, 154
Shakespeare & Company, 33
The Shakespeare Papers
    what are they? 7
    examples of shadowboxes for,
        54, 111, 112, 230
Sharpie pen on acrylic paint, 52
sheets of adhesive, StudioTac, 27
Sheldon
    Greg, 2, 6
    Jered and Larissa Karr, 92
    Lauren Karr, 100, 168
    Zinnie (Zinfandel), 27
shelf-liner resist technique, 101
Shore, Tosya, 75, 78
Sickels, Chris, 193
Sikora, Gaia, 185
Smith, Daniel, watercolors, 17
Sobo white glue, 128
soft body acrylics, 17
Sophisticated Finishes for patina, 42, 43, 134
spackle, spackling paste, 38-41

Speckle Stone spray paint, 181, 182
Speedy-Carve rubber block, 216
splatter the paint, 94-97
sponge the paint, 90-91, 101
    example of sponged paint, 72
spot varnish effect, 164
spray adhesives, how to keep
    the nozzle clean, 28, 129
Spray Mount Artist's Adhesive, 28
stamping, 210-213
    embossed effect with stamps, 164-167
    foam makes good stamps, 103, 213
    make your own stamps, 211
    resist technique with paint, 103-105
    wall stamps are foam, not rubber, 103
    with paper towels, 114-115
stencil brushes, 95
stencils
    counters, how to leave them in, 158
    cutting tool for stencil film, 159
    imprint into handmade paper, 147
    in Nubian villages, 157
    texture with palette knife, 41
stone simulation spray paint, 181
Strathmore papers, 14-15
StudioTac dry adhesive, 27, 128
    useful for collaging small pieces, 131
substrate, what is it? 13
Super 77 multipurpose adhesive, 28, 129
Doan, Susan, 6
swivel knife, 24

T

tack, what does it mean? 28
tape
    as resist for paint, 110-111
    masking tape
        create easy stripes, 110-111
        texturize paper with rub and rag, 55
        texturize paper with tape and washes,
        110-111
temporary adhesives.
    See **low-tack adhesives.**
texture
    why do it, 31, 80
    expose the texture with paint, 50-53
    items with which to create texture, 68
Thornton, Kathy, 3
3M Adhesive Remover Pen, 30
tie-dye paper towels, 114
tissue paper, create texture with, 62

Tollett, John, 2, 65, 109, 195, 198, 201
tools
    bench hook for carving, 222
    burnishing tools, 25
    circle cutters, 24
    embossing tool, 43
    Fiskars fabric scissors, 146
    heat gun, 23
    hot glue gun, 27
    knives and blades, 24
    L-bracket, 211
    linoleum cutting tools, 216
    Making Memories tool set, 135
    Martha Stewart's screw punch, 137
    perforating, 25
    rulers of all sorts, 23
    scoring and folding, 25
    scratch tools, 172
    stencil-cutting tool, 157, 159
    wire brush, 137
    wood carving knives, 222
    Xyron gadgets, 27, 128
tooth, what is it? 13
topper to create fake metallic surface,
    42, 43
tracing images
    graphite paper for transferring
        (or make your own), 21
    time-honored tradition for inspiration, 203
    to use as source material for your own
        illustration, 200
tracing paper
    print on it from a desktop printer, 20, 173
    trace images for your own use, 200
    transfer images to substrate with, 20–21
transfer images
    overview, 226
    heat transfer tool, 21, 216
    paint, create a polymer backing
        to transfer it, 85
    products to transfer with, 226, 228
    to substrates for carving, etc., 20–21
    transfer directly to your substrate, 228–229
    transfer to polymer backing, 227, 229
    transfer to polymer clay, 228–229
    transfer with Lazertran paper, 230
    transfer with packing tape, 231
Twain, Mark, 222

𝒰
UHU Tac plastic adhesive, 29, 128
utility knife, 22, 24

𝒱
Van Ness, David, 6
Vega, Ganeen, 171
Velcro to make stamp blocks, 56–57
vellum
    Bristol board, 15
    originally made from animal skins, 147
    tracing paper, 13
Venice, marbled papers in, 122
Versatex Dispersant, 120, 122
Vick's VapoRub, 46
Vinton, Will, 193
vodka effect on paint, 108

𝒲
wallpaper, textured
    make a print from the wallpaper, 225
    use as a stamp into modeling paste, 41
warped paper, how to flatten it, 123
wash
    what is it? 76, 103
    examples of, 77, 87, 104, 107, 113
    wet-into-wet wash, 52
washi papers
    instead of washi
        use dressmaking tissue patterns, 62
        use paper towels, 115
    tough and durable, 60
    use to create texture, 60–65
watercolor paper, 14, 60
    prime with absorbent ground, 61
watercolors
    what are they? 17
    Dr. Martin's Opaque White, 95
    washes, 76–77, 87, 104, 107, 113
    wet-into-wet wash, 52
wax paper. *See* **freezer paper.**
wax resist technique, 100
Wernicke, Anni, 221
white glues
    Aleene's Tacky Glue, 30
    Elmer's, 128
    PVAs are white glues, 29
    Sobo, 128

Williams
    Cliff, 109
    Jerry, 207, 231
    Ryan, Forged Clothing, 53
    Shannon, 198
wine labels
    examples of, 2, 145, 161
    remove label adhesive, 30
Winsor & Newton
    masking fluid, 98
    watercolors, 17
wood
    aging wood, crackled surface, 34
    transfer images to, 21
wood carving, 222–223
wood engraving
    hold the tool still, move the block, 217
    vs. wood block carving, 206
wooden type
    big beautiful drawer full of, 225
    cast paper letters from, 154
wood pulp paper
    fiber paste paper won't disintegrate, 149
    invention of wood pulp paper, 147
    rag paper is stronger than, 13, 147
    washi is stronger than, 60

𝒳
X-acto knife
    indispensable tool, 24
    swivel blade, 24
Xyron gadgets, 27, 128

𝒴
Yasutomo Nori adhesive, 29
Yes! Paste, 29, 128, 131

𝒵
Zhen, Lian Quan, 78

Rediscover your passion for creativity